GU01019297

They Shine
They Fly
They're Angels

Colleen & Olivia Brady

authorHOUSE™

1663 LIBERTY DRIVE, SUITE 200
BLOOMINGTON, INDIANA 47403
(800) 839-8640
WWW.AUTHORHOUSE.COM

This book is a work of non-fiction. Unless otherwise noted, the author and the publisher make no explicit guarantees as to the accuracy of the information contained in this book and in some cases, names of people and places have been altered to protect their privacy.

First published by AuthorHouse 3/8/2006

ISBN: 1-4208-8540-5 (sc)

Printed in the United States of America
Bloomington, Indiana

This book is printed on acid-free paper.

Golden Light Has Shone Upon Our Irish Home
And Now We Are Going To Shine It Upon Yours!

Colleen & Olivia Brady M.I.R.I

In Loving Memory Of Eileen &
Peter Coney, And Grandparents Agnes &
Joseph Brady. Also Dedicated To Our
parents Oliver & Madeline Brady.

Contents

Preface

As a child my family and I have always attended mass and had strong faith in our Guardian Angels, thanks to our parents who cared enough to carry on their strong belief as Catholics. I have always been fascinated with Angels, Fairies, Unicorns, Mermaids and Leprechauns; as a child your mother will read you magical imaginative stories such as the unforgettable Snow White, Cinderella, Beauty and the Beast, Sleeping Beauty and many others. All along, my sister Olivia and I, had a strong belief that Mermaids and Fairies existed, and no one could tell us any different, if they tried, we'd turn into fierce hot headed Dragons as we are both typical Arians. As we grew older, my sister let her child like personality fade around the age of thirteen. I couldn't understand; why doesn't she want to watch cartoons with me anymore? She was only two years my senior, yet she was growing more mature mentally than I was. When our aunts came down with their children to play with us, Olivia sat in the kitchen drinking tea and eating boring old sandwiches with our aunts instead of playing with us! How unbelievably boring we all thought! But now as we have matured in our years, Olivia's beliefs were always strong as ever, she was just too shy to admit it. As a child she thought when you're thirteen, you had to act all grown up and adult like! Olivia was a secret believer I would say, where as I was an open believer! There's no difference. The connection to our imaginative world was strong as ever. My sister Olivia is a healer and has a business at home, she's a qualified reflexologist and IET practitioner, (Which is Integrated Energy Therapy; similar to the energy of Reiki, but a slightly different connection, to our Lord's messengers the Angels.) So really she brought the connection with the Angels into our home. I was always connected to the Spiritually

Deceased, while Olivia has an Angel connection, which you will discover throughout this book, we hope you enjoy!. Thanks to Doreen Virtue, she has inspired both my family and I, through her writings, and also I'd like to thank Diana Cooper. Through her work, she also has been an inspiration. She has warned us about Lucifer the fallen Angel that once was with God. We thank her, and we hope that they both will read our book one day and say they feel inspired by it, as we have been with theirs! Another Psychic Medium we want to acknowledge, is John Edwards. He proved a real source of Inspiration, when I knew nothing of my connection with the Spiritually Deceased. We would like to take this opportunity to thank our family for their ongoing support. We couldn't have done this without them, they have been behind us all the way. Thanks Daddy for having belief in us from the start, we love you, and we will eventually be able to pay you back all the money you have generously given us! Mummy we love you , your quite the mad little hatter, but hey we wouldn't have a sense of humour today only for you, thank you for our huge personalities! We also have to thank our brother Stephen and his beautiful wife Anita for also having faith in us, your more than just a Sister in law to us, big thanks from us both.   Also we would like to thank our friends for their support and trust. You are the sun that shines bright on cloudy days. Thank you. And last but not least, our two younger sisters Eileen and Kate, we love you girl's! Yes Eileen, you heard that , since you are constantly torturing us for hug's here's one sis, mmmmmmmmmmmwah! Love ya! Kate, you're a little party goer, your wild and your talented, wouldn't have you any other way, (try and ease the temper though!) Don't worry Roisin I haven't forgotten about you! I'd like to take this opportunity to thank my loyal child hood friend Miss Roisin Devlin. We've known each other sixteen years, and even though our friendship has had its ups and downs, we always seem to come through in the end. You're my best friend, and you gave me plenty of practice in my readings in the beginning, so in a way, I wouldn't have gone this far without you! (Thanks Butterfly!) I would also like to thank some of our close friends who are also spiritual workers for Our Lord, such as my sisters boyfriend Mr Nigel Johnson for accepting us and the Angels without hesitation. Your guidance not only as one of our Advisors, but close friend has been much appreciated, your humour has been a healing in our friendship, you've even made us laugh about the biggest problems in our lives turning them only into dust. We have shared many awesome spiritual moments together, there are no words for our gratitude in having such faith in us both and of course our friends the Angels, thank you. (bet he's looking smug now), and also his sister who is our loyal and trusting friend Pauline Johnson. We appreciate your curiosity and positive readings, Thank you for your support and optimism and our many happy social outings! Also Mr Eamonn Cushnahan for your support. We have enjoyed helping widen your horizon of the Angelic and Spirit Realms, its nice to know that we are friends as well as relatives. Also my mothers sisters. Lily, I want to thank you for all those years you have patiently taught me, without you I would never have played the piano for this long and loved every moment of it; only for you inspiring me as a pianist I would never have come this far. Thanks to you, I am probably one of the most calm collected people on Earth, with all those relaxing classical pieces you have taught me with such dedication. Thank you. Secondly my aunt Roisin. Thank you for your faith and helping spread the word of our gift, we are truly grateful; Teresa for introducing me to some of my first decks of cards; our Uncle Anthony Coney, for his faith and trust in us. Your positive expectations are most grateful, without your positive messages which you had obviously received, we would have been at a loss. You dissolved every doubt within us, Thank you. To our other two Aunts Carmel and Bernie, thank you for your support, and interest in this book. Last but not least our only living Grandparent Lucy Coney, Thank you Granny for creating a wonderful person such as mummy. She wouldn't be the person she is without your inspiration. Thankfully Olivia and I have a wicked sense of humour, passed from you onto mummy and with great privilege onto us. Thank you Granny, we love you to pieces! Another close friend of the family that we would like to thank is Philomena (Mena) Carolan, you were one of my early clients and now you are one of many, all thanks to you of course. You informed those who had great faith in their Angels and introduced me to wonderful people like yourself that has appreciated the Angels and my time to no end. Also a huge thank you for having faith in the fluttering experience etc. (for you readers, you shall soon learn later on throughout this book, what the fluttering experience is).   We also want to thank our talented and creative illustrator Peter Hutchinson who's responsible for the front cover of this book.   We can't seem to think of anyone else to thank, so we want to thank all our relatives that support us, don't want to leave anybody out! Finally we would like to thank you, yes YOU for buying our book, and we hope you enjoy. It is all very true, with no fiction what so ever! Even though our lives seem like a roller coaster ride, there is a happy ending! Pray to your Angels and your Deceased loved ones. Just because they're no longer in our world, doesn't mean they aren't with you, because they are! Their world is much more positive and real. So take a cup of tea, coffee, even pour yourself a small glass of wine if you prefer (the reason why I have said small, well I don't want you getting drunk and seeing the font enlarging or waving in all directions) sit back, put your feet up, and lock all the doors, unhook the phone line and follow my sister and I through our fascinating Journey through this life! (So far!)

Acknowledgements

We would like to take this opportunity to thank our most glorious Archangels and Angels. We would also like to thank our Spirit Guides that have lovingly guided us, to take the most positive pathway possible in our lives, Emily, Caroline, Jake, Jelese, Bobby, Lavender, Jaques, Peri, Lana, Moka, Majestic and Neil, you have helped us to no end. We both think its unbelievable how people on the other side can educate you here on Earth. Thank you all!

Olivia and I would also like to thank our Deceased loved ones that have channelled through at various times, with wonderful breathtaking messages, Our aunt Eileen, Grand Dad Coney, Grandparents Joseph and Agnes Brady and our great aunt Cissie, your messages have brought tears of happiness and ongoing joy, thank you!

Chapter 1
A Blessing In Disguise?

As a child I was never like the other children in my class. I suffered three black outs when I was a child and put on medication to treat epilepsy, even though I hadn't been diagnosed with it. At first the doctors thought it was a brain tumor, but thankfully the scan results were negative. My mother gradually stopped giving me my medication after a period of two years as I had only taken three seizures within the first two months and had shown no symptoms since. In fact I have never taken another seizure. The Angels informed me when the connection began that my black outs were a result of information being sent from spirits as they realised the potential of my gift and that I could have been of help to them even as a child. Although this was a negative experience, I still was youthful, humourous and loved to play with other children. Yet there was something missing in my life, like a deep hole formed in my abdomen that needed to be filled. I often sat and cried, but didn't know why, or what I was crying about. It was torture mentally not knowing what was wrong with me, yet I was soon to discover what lurked behind all those emotions, and what provoked such emotion within me was simply a true gift that I hadn't yet discovered. I used to get up in the mornings and appreciate the sun shining bright, the grass sparkling with spring rain, I was only four years old; What four year old does anyone know that has such gratitude for the sun and the rain? Even though I had a roller coaster of emotion when I was a child, I had and still have two wonderful parents; such care and love had I and my family received, none of us were deprived of love or affection. My father is like no other man, and I have respected him from a young age, if you were feeling down my father was the first one to make you smile, my mother is a wonderful caring person. She gave all of us such love at such a young age, I still wonder how she managed, having two toddlers and a baby all at the one time, (that was three diapers to change!). Such work, I don't even think Super mom could accomplish that!. Even though it might sound like I had the perfect childhood, brilliant parents, a house in the country, peace and quiet, receiving anything we needed, clothes, toys, etc, that same hole in my stomach kept irritating me! It was like you had missed your breakfast and went to school on an empty stomach, and we all know what that feels like, don't we ? I never informed anyone of my personal feelings, because I had this fear of my mom bringing me to the doctors. I absolutely dreaded hospitals, doctors and anything to do with being away from home. I didn't even like staying in my friend's or relative's home, when they had invited me to stay over night, I would completely freeze and say "Can I ring and ask my mum?". Well of course I was wishing she would scold me and say no, and my wish was always granted, thanks to my over protective mother, (Thanks mum!)

Those were happy days, when it was just me my older sister Olivia and my older brother Stephen. I was the baby of the household, everything was perfect! Then when I was at the age of four, I remember my mother with this huge belly. I remember distinctly thinking she had a basket ball under her jumper, but my ignorance was soon melted away, as my mother let me touch her belly and see if I could feel the little baby inside. I liked the thought of having a little sister or brother to play with. (My older sister was very mature even though she was only two years my senior; she hated dolls, I loved them, so we didn't quite see eye to eye as children, but now we are very close. She's my best friend I couldn't do without her!). Eventually when my mother went into labour after the very long wait of nine months, which seemed forever as a child, my father had told my sister, brother and I, that we had a new little baby sister. I was very excited, I couldn't wait for my mum to bring her home. Then my father said "I'm taking you all to see your mum and little baby sister in hospital". I froze all over! No way I thought am I going to visit my mother in such a horrible place, I cried, I screamed and kicked. So my father eventually gave up on taking me as I didn't want to go, and I went to my Grandmothers. This continued for the next few days, while my mother was in hospital with my baby sister. She was a few weeks premature and suffered from jaundice. I watched from my Grandmothers house; my father walking hand in hand with my older brother and sister, and I remember thinking " Why are they not scared?" they had big smiles on there faces, and Olivia the mature six year old was all mentally organized to take care of the baby, you might think I don't sound normal as a child, but at least I wasn't a grown woman mentally at the age of six ! (no offence Olivia). Olivia is the total opposite now, over the years as she's got older she actually has gotten more child like, weird huh?. Its like she was putting her shoes on the wrong feet all her life and then sixteen years down the line she thought "Hey this couldn't be right" and changed them to their correct position. Your probably sitting down comfortably with this book in your hands and wondering how can she remember back to four years old? Well I don't think I have to remind you when I say, I wasn't any normal child; my earliest memory was at the age of six months. Yes, you can close your mouth now! (I'm guessing your jaw has dropped?). Don't worry that's normal, everyone's reaction is exactly the same, either that, or I get a big eye roll from a few people which is more or less saying "as if". Now to get back to the big "issue" my younger sister Eileen. She is named after my mothers sister Eileen, that died at the age of seventeen tragically. My aunt Eileen was my Godmother, and I still have a few memories of her, even though she died when I was two years old. I have labelled them my treasured memories, because they are very real, like it was just yesterday and so vivid, its unbelievable. I thank God for letting me save those memory's like a computer would save them on a disc. Again I'm totally off track with my younger baby sister Eileen! Eileen was a 10lb 7oz baby, your probably thinking WOW and she was premature!!? Yes that's correct. My younger baby sister was humongous, and she was a different skin colour from us. I thought my mother had bought her at the hospital as at that age I didn't know about the birds and the bees, your probably wondering why I'm giving you such detailed information about this enormous baby? Right? Well when that huge baby came into my life I thought she was a living hell, she cried, but mostly laughed, and everyone smiled at her little chubby face and her little black curly locks! I was so devastated when everyone's eyes were on the so called baby Eileen, I was wondering why I wasn't the main attraction in my family's life anymore. That's when I came more in tune with the Heavenly Dimension, because I wasn't the main attraction anymore, I needed to focus my active brain onto something else, so I'd sit every morning before I'd go to play school, and watch the TV programme called Bewitched. I was fascinated in the way she would twitch her nose and instantly receive things and go places, anything she wanted she got! I thought great I've got the answer now, I could vanish this huge baby that was destroying my childhood, But of course sadly at the time it didn't work as she is still present in my life and I thank the Lord for not letting my powers vanish her, she's a humorous funny person and quite mature for her age, and I wouldn't have it any other way!

Now finally I get to introduce to you my little sister Kate. She is now the baby of the family; I am twelve years her senior and she is a treasure. Strangely she is very like me, the active mind with the larger-than-life personality; the little attention seeker, the one that could play forever. I was exactly the same, and when I look at her I see myself reflecting back, I thank the Lord for not having me as the youngest in my family, as it wouldn't have been much fun. Now my fun will last much longer with my two younger sisters!

I have left my brother Stephen to the last, as men all know "ladies first". My brother is three years older than me and he is the eldest of the family. He is the one that everyone depends on for support, and Stephen it isn't financially! Ha ha. Even though he gave me money whenever I needed it, when I was a young teenager in High School which is about six years ago, I still hear about all the cash he gave me! I thank him as it topped up my mobile phone, he is an inspiration to me and my family, we lean on him for support; he is our rock! Thanks bro!

Now that I've introduced all my family, it is time to take the Journey though my life. Your probably wondering what exactly is this book about? Well here's some good news. The secret is to be revealed in my next chapter, so enjoy!. I have enjoyed writing the first chapter even though I'm suffering from the cold at the moment, I have laughed, sneezed, coughed etc all through writing this. (Sounds very appealing doesn't it?!) Don't worry I didn't sneeze over your book, just my computer, excuse me while I get some tissues!

Chapter 2
When everything came reality

It all began when I was a child as I told you before, but then I mentally shut the connection off to the Heavenly Dimension because I was frightened, and when fear seeps in, the connection is shut off just like you would switch your bedroom light off. So I continued the rest of my years as a normal child like everyone else. Yet little did I know it was all going to kick start again, only this time around it was twice as powerful!. I was a young teenager at the age of fourteen, it was in the month of June when my relatives from England came to visit, and my mother had got me this beautiful little grey mongrel dog as a pet. As I am an animal lover, my dogs always seemed to fill that annoying void in my stomach that kept making me feel empty. I loved playing with them, giving them attention, and making them feel loved; it gave me such on-going joy! As all Clairvoyants and spiritual workers know, animals are very much in tune with the Heavenly Dimension; little did I know that by doing so, I was steadily opening up my third eye. Its only now I'm realising that the empty feeling in my stomach could only be filled with the positivity that helping others brings.

My first spiritual experience as a teenager happened when I received my little mongrel puppy Pepper. He was only four weeks old, his mother had neglected him, and I got a phone call that I could take him home, as long as I fed him eight times a day. As you can imagine, that meant I had to set my alarm clock to go off during the night, get up make his powdered puppy milk, and feed him through a syringe.

(which I was more than happy to do, as I loved the fact that this little helpless creature needed me). I kept him at my bedside in a cardboard box as it would be much easier for me to attend to him; of course my elder sister Olivia just hated the fact of this puppy being in our room, as she has a fear of animals but since Pepper was so little and harmless ,(he had no teeth, and his eyes hadn't opened yet) she thought "hey why not"! So on the third night of keeping my little puppy by my bedside, I heard him yelping like he was frightened or sensed something he didn't like. I was a little taken back by this, because he hadn't made any noise any of the nights before. Then suddenly my lava lamp at my beside kept clicking on and off, and my electrical fan had turned on at full speed. Well I was so frightened I couldn't move, I just lay there in my bed paralysed with fear. I nudged my sister Olivia, but of course she was pleasantly sound asleep and either didn't hear me, or ignored me, so I lifted my puppy and carried him downstairs. I could hear breathing behind me, and footsteps which weren't far behind my own , so I went into my mother's room crying and shaking with fear. I told her what had happened. She believed me and let me sleep in her room , so I got into her bed. Suddenly this object came out of nowhere at speed, like it was thrown in anger, and hit the wall above my mother's bed. We didn't pay any attention to it out of fear of knowing what it was; my mother just told me to close my eyes and go to sleep. I was really glad to see daylight when I woke up early the next morning to feed my helpless puppy, so after I fed him I thought about the flying object that came into the room . I was curious of what it was, so I went down to my mother's room and looked behind her bed. There it was, a little toy elephant which had been upstairs with the rest of the toys. I thought how did that get down here? It terrified me to think of a ghost throwing an object at me. Did it want to attack me ? Did I do something wrong?. I didn't understand. why me? I thought, I'm a nice person, I pray and attend mass weekly. My mother didn't like to discuss the matter too much the next day, as she was in shock of what happened the night before. She had a little one-to-one conversation with my sister Olivia about the incident. Olivia was really shocked. She found it hard to believe, but yet she was open minded and accepted it, her only question she asked about the frightening experience was "Why didn't you wake me up?". I sighed as I answered her and told her that I tried but she didn't respond at the time. A unnerving feeling had overcame her ,especially as she was in the room with a ghost. She wasn't looking forward to her night sleep that night as you can imagine, who would?. I was so terrified I didn't sleep in my room for two months, I slept on my mothers bedroom floor. Nothing happened for a few weeks after that. I thought great I'm free, no one wants to haunt me anymore! So I went back upstairs to my bedroom and my sister Olivia was pleased as she had missed me. It was fine, I had a great nights sleep with no disturbance. Then suddenly early in the morning, my sister and I were awakened by really loud music from our stereo. It was at full volume, with the CD function on , (and at track number five!). This particular stereo hadn't even been on!. Thankfully it wasn't as terrifying as my last experience, and this time my sister had experienced it with me. The music had actually woke her up, a miracle I thought! This time I wasn't alone. It seemed obvious that the ghosts or spirits were trying to deliver a message to my sister and I.

Olivia and I were innocent and naïve as we were young teenagers; it was only later I learned that spirits and ghosts are often attracted to the powerful energy of some teenagers as they go through puberty. Your puberty years can be a moody, physically challenging, and very confusing time in most teenagers lives.   But not to worry parents, your teenagers aren't all going to be attacked by spirits and ghosts. There are only certain individuals that receive a strong link to the Heavenly Dimension, and if any of them do, it is a gift that God has blessed you with. If you happen to be such a soul, appreciate it. There are a lot of advantages to being one of God's blessed children, as you will soon learn further on in this book. By the way I hope your enjoying it, don't put it down you could miss something! ☺

I hope your questioning yourself about the way I differentiate between ghosts and spirits. You might think they are all one and the same. Well let me tell you, they are very different energies. Ghosts are people that have lived on our planet, and when they died, they didn't want to go to God's light. It doesn't mean they have an evil energy; it means that they are afraid of being judged!. Our Lord doesn't judge you when we pass over to the Heavenly Dimension, we place ourselves in a location in the after life. If we feel we have carried out wrong deeds and experience guilt, we will receive a punishment because of it. This terrifies people when I say this, but it is only common sense. If you are a person that has attended our Lord's home regularly, and actually pay attention to what your priest or preacher is saying, you will be rewarded in Heaven; if you are a person that attends church and daydreams about all sort of things, or make comments on the dreadful jumper the woman in front of you is wearing, well you are committing a sin directly under the crucifix!. Why attend God's home when your sinning before the priest and most importantly Our Lord. That sin would be displayed to you when you pass over! If you are one of these people, don't panic, I can save you! Start attending your church and listening, say your night and morning prayers with thought and devotion, and ask for God's forgiveness.

He will never reject you; there is a place in the Heavenly Dimension for everyone! So I'd advise you to either attend Church and listen, or do not attend and pray with thought at home. Do not sin when your under Our Lord's crucifix, and think no one knows it. Let me tell you people, Our Lord receives and knows every single thought!. Now I don't want you to go all crazy or paranoid over every bad thought you have. As we are all human, we have an emotional side.

We experience anger, laughter and sadness; Our Lord knows this, and takes this into account as part of our human nature. I have received this information from one of Our Lord's messengers, YES I HAVE A CONNECTION WITH ANGELS!!!, I'm full of surprise's aren't I ? At just the age of twenty, I am a medium clairvoyant. Let me explain the meaning of clairvoyance to you. There are three different areas of "clairs". There are medium clairvoyants, who can see and hear deceased people; there are clairvoyants, who are psychic (they can only hear spirits, they cannot see them); there are also clairsentients, who can `sense` if a spirit is around, without any other form of contact with them, and last but not least, there is also the clairaudient, who has the power of hearing and knowing about sounds beyond the range of the normal human range. This means that the clairaudient can actually hear the deceased person's voice. I can hear their voices but not physically. I only can hear their thoughts. It was difficult receiving their thoughts in the beginning ,but now I can hear them very clearly. As my aunt Lily used to say in my piano lessons "Practise makes perfect". She is clearly correct on that phrase! There's another little surprise, I'm a classically trained pianist! I have been playing the piano from the age of six. The Angels always advise spiritual worker's to listen to classical music to relax their mind; they didn't have to advise me, as I was playing it all the time. Apparently it makes the connection stronger to the Heavenly Dimension, which I have full faith in. Any spiritual workers I know either play an instrument or listen to music frequently!

This is when I realised that everything that was happening to me was reality. It was real. I wasn't hearing voices that weren't there, they were deceased people wanting to be heard and I had to help them! So my mother got me a deck of Tarot card's in 1998 thinking that it would help me along the process, they were beautifully illustrated, except for one card.. the Devil! Yes you heard me, I said the Devil. It was the most unbelievably ugly face I had ever seen! I wanted to replace it from the deck rip it up and throw it in the fire, but I couldn't as it was a part of the deck. When I was learning the meanings of the cards, I tried to avoid learning the meaning of the "Devil" so I left it to the last, and it was easy to do so as there were over seventy cards in the deck. Eventually when it came to the Devil card, I learned that it wasn't so evil. It had many meanings. It could either mean an engagement, or an oncoming change in a person's life, so I used my family as guinea pigs and practised on them, (doing their Tarot card readings of course). I had the book with the card's meanings out endlessly!. I didn't seem to connect with them. Whenever I did a reading, I wasn't getting message's from deceased people like I had gotten before, so I gave up. I had received many deck's of Tarot card's since that year, and still I couldn't connect with them. I thought maybe I'm just not gifted enough. That's when the doubt started to seep in. So my negative thought's blocked off my gift from God, thankfully not forever! I received it just last year in the month of August 2003. My mother bought me these beautifully illustrated cards. They were nothing like the cards I had before, they were all positive,

and guess what? Thankfully there was no ugly faced Devil!.
(Thank you Lord I thought to myself!). I connected to these
brightly illustrated cards immediately as soon as I opened
them! They were my connection to the Heavenly Dimension,
and that's when my door which had been locked for a few
years, suddenly sprang open with one big jolt, and obviously
this time I threw away the key,.... who wouldn't?

Chapter 3
Who's calling us?

So here I was with my beautifully illustrated cards, and again using my family as guinea pigs to do readings!. They didn't mind, they were getting very precise readings. Of course I had to study the meanings at first, but after all the practise I received, I became a qualified card reader!. Yeah sounds snazzy doesn't it?! My sister Olivia was really intrigued by them, and so was my good friend Roisin, although I think it has became more of an addiction for her! (I'm going to get a right slap over the head for saying that, or maybe she'll buy me a drink? What do you think?). I had done several readings with my family at first; my father, brother and sisters of course, but I always seemed to get more of a kick out of reading my mothers cards. There was so much information coming through. It came so rapidly, and better still it was all correct!. My sister Olivia used to say its because she knows more dead people! She was envious; I used to hear "Why isn't anyone that has passed over coming through to talk to me?". It isn't the everyday thing you would hear someone state, longing to hear messages from the deceased! (But then again my house isn't the ordinary Irish home!) After I had finished my private piano lessons one evening around 8.00pm, my mother asked me to do a reading, and as usual I didn't refuse. I loved doing readings, especially as I was becoming more accurate every time. So I went down to Olivia's holistic healing room, retrieved my cards, and took them up to the kitchen. I sat down opposite my mother at the table. She shuffled the cards to place her energy into them. She took seven out of the deck and placed them on the table. I didn't even get time to read the cards before I got an instant eager voice in my mind saying "tell Madeline its me". I told my mother what I had received. She couldn't think of who it could be, so I asked the Spirit to give me some information to reveal their identity. Whoever this deceased person was, they were being very polite and co-operative. I was sensing a feminine energy, so I knew instantly it was a young woman. She give me a few pictures which I thought looked like a slide show, one after the other moving very quickly. I had seen a pair of shoes in a grey box that seemed to be brand new, and a mouth with someone sticking their tongue out. My mother gasped!. "Its Eileen" she said instantly! (My aunt that died in the tragic accident as I mentioned earlier, you with me?) The reason why she was displaying the image of the shoe box ,was because she worked in a shoe shop, and the person sticking out their tongue was her. The night she had died, she was asked by the paramedic if she could hear him to respond by sticking her tongue out, and she had! Of course I never knew that information as it was many years ago. Eileen came in very clearly that night. She gave several different images that referred back to my mother, such as she drank black coffee, wore little black pump shoes, hated her feet; the dying of her hair the night before she died, and even an image of her boyfriend at the time. I was able to describe him from head to foot; the clothes he wore, everything!. It was amazing! My mother was over whelmed and she thanked Eileen for coming through and giving her a message that she was happy and watching over us! After that reading I was mentally drained, as I was only new to this, and I had to use full concentration to receive her messages, but it was worth it. I was really shocked that night because I was so accurate on the thoughts I was receiving. I had never known of any of the information my aunt Eileen was delivering to me, and that's when my mother knew that this was reality. She realised that this was a gift and she hugged and thanked me. Ever since, I've had many visits from a number of my mothers deceased relatives. You will receive all of this information throughout this book, so be patient! Take deep breaths! Calm your excitement!

My sister Olivia, who is also very intuitive, would also receive some thoughts when I was reading for my mother or my friends. We are great at working together, because when I receive vibrations of information from the higher Dimension, I sometimes don't receive everything, as it comes in at such a fast speed. Its like a computer downloading information from the internet, only we're downloading information into our minds. Therefore, when they send this to me, it either inserts the information into the right side of my brain where I receive all messages, or it bounces off my energy and inserts itself into Olivia's brain, and she receives the message. So that way the message is being totally delivered the way it is supposed too.

I don't think many of us know how powerful the human mind really is, it is so intelligent! Take a moment and think of our bodies. They're like a protective suit; we're in it, and it looks after us, when we take an infection it fights it off as best as it can, it lets us know when were ill etc etc, how intelligent is that?!. Here Olivia and I are at the ages of twenty and twenty two, and we have a very strong connection to the Heavenly Realm!. We are barely out of our teen years, and yet we have developed a connection to Gods messengers, the wonderful glorious Angels whom we respect exactly like we would respect Our Lord. When we receive a message from any of the Angels that Olivia and I have had experience with, we don't think of it just coming from the Angels, we know they convey Our Lords comforting words. I like to think of it as Our Lord is their tutor and the Angels are his students, listening to all his guidance and advice. They are like our mailmen here on Earth, only they can travel at a much faster speed. (They travel by light and thought. If only our mail could arrive like that huh!! Could you handle your mailman delivering your mail maybe at the bottom of your bed! I don't think any of us would want that, with bad morning breath and a hideous night dress or pyjamas and your hair standing straight up on your heads! I am pleased that our world is different! Aren't you?)

There are many Angels. They all are very close to Our Lord. They are like his employees, only they are not given a wage and they're still loyal! Imagine having employees like that!. If you own your own business and your reading our book, I'm guessing you're feeling a little envious about this concept? Don't worry, we're all human, we can get a little jealous at times. Our Lord's messengers were first introduced to Olivia and I about six years ago. We would hear our names being called by these calm soothing voices; we thought our mother was calling us but then we thought "nah that doesn't sound like her". So, have you had an experience where you hear your name being called by a beautiful soothing voice, like you would hear in a religious movie? Well if you have, we are here to calm your mind. You are not hearing things ! Your mind is definitely not playing up, it is very real. Your Angels are letting you know that they are here, caring for you, and guiding you through your life. We have all different pathways to choose from, and our Guardian Angels will always try to guide us down the right path! So thanks to them, Olivia and I are writing a book, and letting the world know that Angels do exist in a very real way. They are becoming more known now all over the world, so believe in them, they help everyone of us so much! We couldn't do without them; they are our companions from birth our tutors, and our guides. Not even Our Lord could do without them, and they certainly wouldn't exist without him. Thank you God!

If you have had an experience with an Angel , may it be that you have heard or even caught sight of an Angel, and you would like to satisfy your curiosity and learn more, follow the exercise below and relax your mind, open your minds eye, and who knows what you may receive, good luck!

- **Put on soothing meditating music.**
- **Clear your mind of all thoughts.**
- **Sit comfortably on a chair with your hands on your knees, and legs firmly on the floor so you are grounded.**
- **Close your eyes.**
- **Imagine a wonderful golden light surrounding your body. You are in a safe place and no negative energies can attack you, as you have your golden light protecting you.**
- **Pray for a time with devotion and thought.**
- **Ask for the assistance of your Angels.**
- **You may see colours forming. That means your minds eye is clearing.**
- **Spend about 30mins doing this, relaxing your mind.**
- **You will feel refreshed and feel much more relaxed each time you are done.**
- **Each time you meditate you become more in tune with the Angels.**

If you are a person who cannot relax, not to worry, I have another form of meditation, ALLEUIA your probably screaming! Yes we can help you. If you are a gifted painter or an artist of any kind (It may be musically or whatever), sit everyday and practise the art, your minds eye will open and you will be more in tune. If you aren't musically talented or artistic do not fret! You can light a candle in a dim room, and gaze at the flickering flame. This also cleanses your minds eye. Sit for at least 15mins studying the flame and close your eyes every few minutes. Little glowing bubbles will then form. If you have difficulty seeing any of the above do not worry, it takes time to develop this; keep practising and it will improve, it's a fact and it has been proven! Personally, I was never one for meditating, so I would play my favourite classical pieces. My sister would do both sometimes. She would put relaxing classical music on, or play her traditional fiddle (Violin). Everyone has different forms of meditation. Whatever you enjoy, even if you love walking out in the country, or listening to the sounds of nature in the park, its all a form of meditation! So remember, if you have heard or even caught sight of an Angel, you could have a hidden gift that wants to burst out. You're the only one that has the key. Think about it. If you meditate enough, pray and ask for the highest of good, you will receive answers, you aren't being called upon for nothing!

Chapter 4
Do Cats Really Have Nine Lives?

What is your verdict on past lives? My gut feeling tells me its the same as mine! My mother used to attend psychic classes about two years ago. She was curious about the unknown, and since her mother used to read playing cards and tea leaves, I guess she was always open minded about it.(I managed to open her doorway that little bit further!). My mother would come home every Sunday of the month, and tell Olivia and I about her experiences. Past lives was a topic in one of the classes. My mother was told by one of the tutors that she was a Nun in the 18th Century; she agreed, and could relate to what she had been told. I remember laughing in disbelief thinking you could tell anybody anything about their past lives, as there is no evidence of it actually happening. My laughter of ignorance soon came to an end. A few weeks later, I was sitting at my kitchen table when suddenly I was in a whole different room and atmosphere. It was like I had emigrated to America, and turned back the hands of the clock leaving me in the 1800's! There were people everywhere carrying out their every day duties; there were horses, carriages, men selling newspapers, I couldn't believe it!. The men were dressed in short jackets and waistcoats with pocket watches, while the women wore long dresses with feathered hats, and a little black man was shining shoes across the street from where I was standing!. It was like I was in a movie, I could feel a warm breeze on my face. Then people began to address me with   " hello how are you Pearl?". I looked over my right shoulder and to either side of me wondering who they were talking to. Suddenly,

I was taken back into the comfort of my own home, with my mother in front of me cooking dinner. I said to her, "Did you see any of that?" She just looked at me, and said "See what?". I said "The carriages, the horses….".Then I just froze. "Oh my God" I said, "I think I've just experienced one of my past lives!" My mothers ears suddenly pricked up as if to say your talking sense now! I told her all about it and she loved every minute of hearing about my past live experience!

I hadn't received any Spiritual messages for a few weeks before that unforgettable experience. It was like I was being sent a message saying, "Hey there are such as things as past lives, and we are going to prove it". Of course I had total faith in past lives after that, who wouldn't? I guess seeing is believing. At first I was sceptical when I first heard of past lives. (Definitely not now though!). So if you ever dream of being in a different country, and it seems to be back a few centuries, it is not your imagination!. You are experiencing one of your lives on Earth! Yes you heard me, one of your lives! You could have up to one hundred different lives, (I bet the Cats are envious now!!)

Another thing I have learned about past lives, is that if you have experienced something negative in a life before your present life now, you can actually carry it on emotionally and even physically!. I will give you an example. One evening I had received a phone call from a woman that seemed to be in her late forties. She seemed quite eager for an appointment! Sensing fear in her voice, I agreed to take her as soon as I could. Three days later as I was preparing the room for her arrival, I felt great sadness as I began lighting candles for this client. I knew it definitely wasn't a personal sadness of my own. It seemed to be of disloyalty, yet I couldn't quite pin point what it was. Just at that, I heard a vehicle approach the front drive of the house, so I put that thought in a box in the back of my mind. As I greeted this woman at my front door that evening, her eyes looked strained and she seemed lacking in self love. I immediately knew that this reading was going to be indeed quite deep; she seemed to have gone through many battles. I gazed at the cards which lay before me on the table, remaining as relaxed as I possibly could, to calm her nervousness. My client sat in the chair before me as if she had no tomorrow; her eyes were so lost as she stared at me, searching my face for help and advice. Reading her cards, I had saw that there was no communication in her relationship; it seemed to be all one sided,(but not from her husband). I remember thinking she couldn't be at fault within her marriage. I was wrong to doubt what I was receiving as it was very accurate! As I spoke to her, telling her of what I seen, she agreed, as her tears flowed with guilt. Her face conveyed her worry, she asked me "why am I like this? My husband loves me, but yet I cannot have him touch me". This woman sat there before me, wondering why she feared sexual relations with the man she loved dearly, when she had told me of never being sexually or mentally abused in any way. I then informed her of her past lives, and how they can affect you, even in your present life. I noticed she began to relax with this piece of information; I knew she hoped that she could have the answer to the blockage in her marriage that evening. As I soon discovered, she had had a terrifying experience. In the late 1700's, she was sexually abused by six men, as she was walking home alone from a party at her neighbours. This caused so much turmoil in her life, that she ended up drowning herself to end her torture, having never spoken of it. My client could totally relate to this. Not only did it explain her sexual inhibitions, but also, whenever she was near water, she could feel her stomach curdle with fear. The Angels did not only help her clear one blockage but two! Now that her mind was set at ease and the Angels had cleansed her soul of fear, she walked out the front door of my home happy and confused no more. A few weeks later my client contacted me, informing me of her new-found healthy relationship with her husband. A new door way had opened for her, and she was experiencing true love for the first time, with trust in her partner that he would never hurt her. This is only one experience that I have shared with you, there are many more. Are you confused, or have a debilitating phobia that hinders your life?. There is always a reason for everything, it is not just because you are a wimp, it is because behind every door there is a pathway, no matter where it may lead to, there is always an ending or better still, a beginning. If you want your Angels to help......just ask!

I suppose your thinking I can bring people into deep hypnosis ? Well no, I haven't conquered that task yet. However, through time maybe I will. At the moment, I can read into peoples past lives for them, and tell them what they were and what the date is. I haven't done this on anyone other than my family and a few friends. I think the situation may prove too extreme for most people to sit and watch, as I go into a trance and don't seem to register that my own world exists. So I decided no matter how open minded a person is, I could not let them see how I react going into their past lives, its not a pretty sight. I sweat with fear, I laugh , I talk, I basically look crazy! So I think its best not to, wouldn't you agree?

There is one specific past life that I have went into for my sister Olivia, and it has been on my mind a lot. I think its because it was such a positive past life I have never forgotten it, but I also think its because I didn't get to ever finish it, and its left me curious. I have tried endlessly to place myself back into it; unfortunately it has never occurred. I will explain to you generally of what happened, but I shall disappoint you when I say there is no ending. You may need a box of tissues near hand you as you will cry your eyes out; it starts so brilliantly, yet ends so sad…don't worry we can get through this, deep breaths!

Olivia and I were sitting at our kitchen table. I had just given her a reading, and she then asked me to go into one of her past lives. (Of course I didn't hesitate, who would?) So I cleared my mind, and asked by thought for an image of one of Olivia's happy positive past lives. Suddenly, I was running through a wheat field. I saw this person running not far in front of me; she had long curly black hair, and was wearing a beautiful white dress with red imprinted roses on it. It seemed like a ball gown; she had one shoe in her hand, and her hair bounced as she ran. I decided I would catch up with her to see who she was. I looked up at the sky and there wasn't a cloud in sight, it was so blue and peaceful. I looked down at myself to see if what I was wearing. I also had one of these dresses on. A beautiful ball gown in lemon with a dark yellow band under the breast line. It was stunning, and so long, that I had to lift it up really high as I ran. At first I thought she was running from me, then she said " hurry up they're going to catch us". I thought to myself, who? There was only the two of us in this vision, so I decided to turn around and see who was chasing us. To my surprise there were two handsome men there, who seemed to be in their mid-twenties, running after us in a playful manner.......
Then I heard a noise, and I found myself at the table looking upon Olivia, who by now had become so curious as to what I could see. I was so angry.   I'm a big fan of fairy tales, and this was like Cinderella, only with me in it! Yes that is it. I have no happy ending for you. Sad isn't it. Don't cry to much, maybe if you pray for me to receive the image again, God might send me the image once more. (I'll let you know the happy ending in my next book!)

If your feeling sceptical about past lives, its totally understandable. I was a sceptic myself, but seeing is believing. You may receive one in a dream, or even watch a movie and find the whole setting familiar; there are countless ways to `Tap in` to past lives. When you get this feeling (like Déjà vu; you could be on holiday and you don't feel homesick, or get the feeling you've lived there before), ask yourself why do I feel so at home? Well I have the answer for you. You were there before! Yes, you heard me! Think about it. Don't just try and argue your point yet. It makes perfect sense. The world is enormous; Earth is a huge planet with many countries, one of which you live in now. Now, when you die, do you feel that you have experienced everything that this fabulous planet has to offer? In your one life on this huge place? Well answer me! Would you? Of course you wouldn't! You would want to go back again and again to experience more to satisfy your soul! Why die unhappy and unfulfilled, when you can go back again for a holiday and carry out all that you have not yet experienced. Eventually when you die, your soul will be fulfilled, and you will have served your time on Earth. You will have carried out every duty your heart has desired, and your heart would then be content. It wouldn't crave this place anymore, so your soul would be free and you could pass onto the Heavenly Dimension, to be with God, the Angels, and all of your relatives that have passed over. You would now be ready to enter a more realistic world, where everyone speaks by thought, and everywhere is full of love. You would travel by light and by thought. It may seem like fiction, but here is the interesting part....... it is all reality!

Chapter 5
When I started sketching like an Artist!

When I was at High school doing my exams, I didn't take on art as one of my subjects. Why you may ask? Well simply because I COULD NOT DRAW! I could only sketch little cartoon characters, and even at that they weren't overly good. My art teacher would give us homework to sketch flowers and fruits and the like. I wouldn't fret because I had the advantage of handing my homework diary to Olivia, who had been blessed with an artistic gift. If I was told to carry out the sketching there and then, I wouldn't have known where to start. (That's why I was always pleased when she said we should do it at home!)

I know what your thinking, I sound like a little cheat don't I ? Oh come on! Like you've never pulled any scams to get your homework done! ☺

It was October of 2003 when I discovered I had an artistic talent. Yip, you heard me! One day Olivia and I were doing some household chores. As I worked, the most beautiful scent of roses came to me. It was like I was standing in a big garden filled with them. I then had this real urge to get a pencil and piece of paper. It was almost like a craving that needed to be satisfied! So I went and got a piece of paper and pencil, sat down at the kitchen table. Before I could even put the pencil onto the paper, I noticed my hand sketching and moving on its own before my very eyes. I had no control over my right arm. I was astonished and sitting in amazement, as my arm was freely moving over the piece of paper sketching and smudging like a true artist. Whatever was moving my hand I thought, knows exactly what it wants to draw! Olivia came over to the table, and stood over my right shoulder. She said "That looks lovely, but you can't draw!". I totally agreed with her, whilst my hand was sketching freely and out of my control. I could feel an energy flow through my arm. It felt so light and tingly all down my right hand; it was such a peaceful feeling. Then I sensed that the drawing was coming to an end as the strong energy flowing through my right arm began to fade slowly. Suddenly my hand stopped; the pencil rolling out between my thumb and fore finger and across the table. I sat and looked at the page in total awe. There before me was this beautifully sketched rose with amazing detail, you could see every petal, and every thorn. There were beams of light coming from the rose, shining so bright. The whole thing looked so vividly realistic that you felt you could just put your hand onto the page and pick the rose up! I called my mother in to see what I had drawn. (Of course she stated "Olivia must have had drawn that, you can't draw" and again I answered I know I can't, you know the story!). I then explained to her what had happened, the wonderful sensation of energy flowing down my arm, and my hand moving freely and lightly on its own, she was intrigued and amazed. I didn't quite know what the rose meant at that stage, but I always related roses to Our lady. I had a hunch

that I was correct, as I had got the scent of roses in the kitchen minutes before the drawing of the rose was even sketched!

I sat that whole day thinking about the drawing of the rose. I'd pick it up, look at it, then put it down again, and I thought to myself where did that come from? I had never heard of anyone's hand sketching on their own before, and out of their control, have you ? Well you have now! I was very confused, but yet I really wanted it to happen again.

As I said my prayers that night as usual I asked God to give me a sign of who it was sketched such a beautiful piece of art. The next morning I had forgotten all about the sign I had asked for, and began doing my usual household chores. When I had finished, I put on the kettle to make a cup of coffee for Olivia, my mother and I. I had just sat down at the table to drink my coffee, when I had this craving to get a pencil and paper again! Of course I dropped everything, and went straight into my fathers office to get some paper. I

sat down again at the table and held the pencil in my hand. A sudden rush of warm energy began flowing down my arm and giving me that tingling sensation once again! So there I was, with the pencil in hand, my piece of paper, and of course this amazing energy force that had taken over my hand, sketching away at speed. As before, I had my mother and my sister Olivia staring over my right shoulder, once again, staring in amazement! I was sitting like a little child ready to open a present to see what was inside, as I was sitting in complete anticipation wondering what would appear on the page before me. Then the energy in my arm again started to fade and drift away. I knew then that the sketching was complete. This one was very different from the last drawing. It was a sketching of an Angel. She had long hair and very innocent eyes, with very large wings behind her; they didn't seem feather like though. She was dressed in a long gown with a girdle around her waist. She was holding Rosary Beads, and she had a bright light surrounding her; she was beautiful and looked so realistic, it was amazing to see! Her eyes were so real, it was like we were being drawn into them. They gave all of us a feeling of love and happiness (Imagine getting that feeling from a drawing?). It was almost like you were being hypnotised, but of course you weren't! We all felt drawn towards them. It was a sketching that you could sit and gaze at all day. I then remembered that I had asked God for a sign of where I was receiving this wonderful uncontrollable artistic energy from. I knew right away that my answer was right in front of us. This beautifully illustrated Angel with her Rosary Beads; She was the one that had sketched these extraordinary images! This was indeed an extraordinary energy force. The images that I was receiving, had a meaning behind them. The sketching of the rose for example. As I had said before, I related the rose with Our Lady, and now I had a sketching of an Angel. The two pictures seemed to fit into place like two pieces of a jigsaw puzzle; Our lady is the Queen of Angels and she was delivering messages to me through them!

My mind was at peace. I knew where this glorious information was coming from, I didn't have to question it any longer! After a few days, the Angels were visiting me more often. I wasn't just getting one picture a day , I started to receive two! Yes that's correct I said two, I know, I was shocked also! ☺

The drawings I received were very positive and optimistic. They were mainly about Our Lord, Our lady, and of course their messengers the Angels.

I would get up every morning, and look over the messages I had received. It all seemed so miraculous. I had to pinch myself every now and again to see if it was really happening, and of course it was! One evening, Olivia and my mother were discussing the drawings. I hadn't received any that whole morning and I was a little disappointed, as I enjoyed the drawings and the positive experience they had brought. I was thinking about all this as we were discussing the drawings. Again, I had the sudden urge to retrieve a pencil and piece of paper. (Thankfully, I thought to myself, I thought you all had forgotten about me!) So I sat down at the table once again, and once again, my hand started to move itself. When the Angels had finally finished the drawing,

I studied what they had done. The drawing was of planet Earth, with someone's body lying down, with a water tap dripping onto the body, and a hand was holding the Earth, like we would hold a tennis ball. I have to say, that at the time I was mystified with this drawing. I thought to myself "What does this mean?", so I asked for some help from the Angels. (They of course never hesitate to help you, they sent the information instantly!) They explained the drawing as follows: The hand that was holding planet Earth was Our Lord signifying that He as the creator of the universe, controls our planet, and looks after it. The person with the dripping tap above their head, was Our Lord trying to satisfy everyone's thirst, in other words everyone's problems.

I had many different drawings over the weeks that followed. I am sharing with you the ones that I was told to share with you, in other words, the most important messages! (Again as per-usual, I sat at the table blah blah blah, as you all know by now, and the magical pictures began once again). This drawing was of a woman's face. She had curly shoulder length hair, with some type of turban like object on her head, which had a jug with little stars pouring out of it. At the right side of her, was a cord of a telephone wire and the bottom of a phone receiver. To the left of it was a beautiful swan with its wings spread, and to the right of the swan was a cross of God, and a heavenly pair of an Angels wings beside it. The meaning of this drawing was very clear. I was the curly haired woman with the head dress; the phone cord was their way of telling me that I had a connection to something, the cord being beside the cross and the Angel wings. So basically, their message was, that I have a strong connection with the Angels; the swan indicated my sister Olivia, as she was to be my student and I was to educate her as she too had this powerful gift!

My sister Olivia is an Earth Angel. No, she doesn't have wings or a little halo above her head, she is a normal twenty two year old, who loves socialising and is up for a laugh. (In other word's she's a wild Irish woman !) I had received the information from the Angels, that Olivia was an Earth angel through their drawings. The Angels had drawn this beautiful bed of sunflowers, and inside one of the sunflowers was a little baby Angel with curly hair, and little wings. There also was an Angel hovering over her, as if it was keeping an eye on things. When I looked at that drawing after it was sketched, I instantly thought of Olivia! But I didn't understand why as the baby Angel looked nothing like her. A few days later, I got another drawing of Olivia as she is now, and she had sunflowers in her hands! That was when it clicked! Olivia is an Earth Angel! When I told her this , she laughed and said "No way, how could I be". I had never even heard of Earth Angels at this point, and yet there I was, standing before my sister and claiming that she was one! As crazy as it all might sound, I was correct. The Angels informed me, that my sister was once an Angel. She was born on a bed of sunflowers, and only lived in the Heavenly Dimension for eighteen months, as she was curious of planet Earth and wanted to live there. God let her leave her wings behind and start a life as a human on Earth. You might be thinking, Why and how would a little eighteen month old baby come out with such thing? Let me remind you people, that baby wasn't just any little ordinary baby, she was an Angel, as I have mentioned before, in the Heavenly Dimension everyone speaks by thought! So if you have a child, that has been very pleasant from they were born, didn't seek much attention, or care for toys; if they are happy skipping around outside in the open fresh air in the sun shine, take another glance at them. If they have vivid shining eyes and an innocent demeanour, you could be standing before an Earth Angel! Don't worry, you don't have to go out and buy them wings or a little halo; they carry their Angelic energy in their hearts, and they will be there to help you in any situation, good or bad, (just like my Angelic sister Olivia who is there for my family and I!). When material and luxuries don't seem to matter to them, you have given birth to an Angel. Don't be alarmed. It is a blessing, they will never leave your side, and they will grow into fantastic caring people because they 're Heaven sent!

Chapter 6
What Beautiful Handwriting, But Who's Is It?

Have you ever heard of automatic handwriting? Well if you haven't, let me explain. Automatic handwriting is a method of receiving messages from the Heavenly Dimension. You have no control over the movement of your hand (Just like the drawings I told you about in the last chapter!) or over the message you receive. Some people can hear such messages physically; (Which I can also do) however, automatic handwriting is sometimes easier to interpret. You see, it can be very difficult at first to differentiate between who is sending you their thought, and your own thoughts, but when you train your mind into whooshing all your problems and happenings in your life all unto the left side of the brain, sort of like turning a page over, it gradually becomes easier. My sister Olivia was in a relationship which I totally knew she wasn't happy in. She was at first, but then a few months down the line when her partner changed, it was like he became a different person. It was like he didn't care about pleasing her anymore. He had this attitude that turned into "Well hey I've got her now, I don't need to impress her anymore" . My friend Roisin and I, had instantly sensed that he changed, but we didn't say anything for a few weeks, until we could take no more. We thought he is not good for her, she deserves a person who will treat her with the respect and decency she deserves. So we took her aside once when we were out socialising, and said "Olivia he's changed, we want you to finish it, you can do so much better". Of course that didn't go down well as you could imagine. Here she was with her partner and thinking she was in love, it hurt her emotionally that we didn't think he was her soul mate. Roisin and I are honest people; maybe a little too honest at times. We would simply just say to Olivia's boyfriend that he wasn't good enough for her, that he didn't treat her the way she deserved to be treated, and when that began, the outcome was never going to be positive, believe me!

Roisin and I were never friends that interfered (much), but there was something about him that always irritated her. I personally got on with him quite well. I thought he was a good laugh, and even though I was quite fond of him, I thought he was quite a deep thinker. He wasn't as open minded as us girls, but I let it go. I said no more to Olivia, I thought "Hey she has to live her own life", if she loves him she loves him! Six months later Olivia started to notice she wasn't as happy as she was at the beginning of the relationship. She didn't mention any of this to us because she knew we had predicted it, and therefore we would be right about him and she would be wrong! She was clearly unhappy; she didn't have that same big smile, the twinkle in her eye, it no longer existed. In other words, she had changed! She was no longer the little happy Earth Angel, her self esteem was getting lower, she didn't really care about socialising anymore, but yet she didn't want to let go of him. I think her self esteem had gotten that low she thought " I can't do any better, so I'll stick with him for the rest of my life". Olivia's boyfriend probably sounds like a right monster, but he wasn't really one. He was a year younger than Olivia, and yet he had control over the relationship. He didn't listen to her. Sure, they laughed and talked, but he didn't really listen to her, unless he was drinking. He wasn't an alcoholic, I think he just drank so much at the weekends, because it brought him out of his shell. He had some respect for my family and we all got on; there were no problems, yet I couldn't pin point what it was about him.

I had said my prayers as usual every night as I always do, and I had asked God and the Angels for their help, to either bring Olivia and her partner closer together or let them part and go their separate ways. (And hopefully remain friends). I needed to save my long lost sister from what she had turned into! I needed to be her hero because he certainly wasn't. Olivia had much more courage than him, she was this beautifully untouched sunflower before she had met him. She had turned into a dead sunflower with drooping petals, her soil was dried up and she was deprived of the richness of water and sun. A few days later, after I had asked God and the Angels for their help on Olivia's unhappy relationship, I had gotten an urge to get a pencil and piece of paper. Of course I was totally used to this wonderful experience daily, that I instantly knew that there was another picture to be sketched with a wonderful meaning behind it. Guess what?....... I was wrong! I know, can you believe it? I couldn't either!

I sat down at the kitchen table once again with my pencil and notepad, when suddenly I felt a very different energy flowing down my arm. It came in with a very strong powerful force. There was a sincere warmth with the energy, and the tingling sensation was much stronger. Suddenly, the pencil started to move and out of my control, but this time it wasn't sketching a drawing, it was creating this beautiful calligraphy- like handwriting. My hand was moving at such a fast speed, until there was a sentence written on the page..... and then it just stopped. I felt the powerful energy release from my arm, and the ongoing tingling vanished! I looked at the page and I could hardly read what was written. It was joined handwriting and very beautiful, yet I couldn't seem to understand what was written. I called Olivia in and she couldn't understand it either. All the letters such as the W,L,Y, looked all the same. It was almost like a different language, it didn't come across as English at all. (As it turned out I had received the sentence in the language of the Angels themselves!) I asked for the Angel who had written this sentence if they would be so kind to try again, as I couldn't understand it. I had only sent this question by thought. It took no time at all for the powerful energy to move flowingly yet quickly down through my arm, it was like my fingers could almost explode the energy was that powerful and intense. I thought to myself, this has to be a very powerful Angel for to have such a strong energy force. The pencil began to move again without my control, and this time it was in English. I thought thank God, now I can read it. Again, it was beautifully written the same style of calligraphy and again the letter's W,Y,L all seemed to be written the same, they were almost moving like waves across the page.

The energy whooshed away from my arm. It wasn't as pleasant as the other Angel who had drawn through me. I could sense her energy fade away slowly; the tingling would fade slightly, and then it would be totally gone. This was different. It was like this Angel had no time. It was almost like a rushed energy, yet I felt very calm and positive. I was sensing a masculine energy from this Angel; he was strong and powerful, almost like he was a knight or some kind of royalty. It seemed like he was even higher in the Heavenly Dimension than the other Angels. So the writing was now in English, it still took me sometime to make out this small sentence, as it was all joined and every letter was so elegantly entwined with the next. I called my mother into the room as she is quite good at understanding others handwriting (she worked as secretary in many office's when she was younger) My mother then called each word out. It stated "Olivia you are trapped, I am saving you from this door closing, and locking on you forever" This message for Olivia, of course, didn't relate to anything else in her life other than her boyfriend. My mother looked at her, and said "Why are you getting a message like that?" Olivia just shrugged and said "I don't know", but secretly the message Olivia received, made a lot of sense to her, as she was trapped. She was trapped in a relationship in which she couldn't express her true self, yet she was so afraid to leave him. She had gotten herself so caught up in a rut of being in this relationship, that she thought she couldn't get out of it unless she had a good reason. Imagine, she thought that if she stayed with him long enough, then someday if he did something really bad to her, she would eventually leave him, as it wouldn't look so stupid leaving him for "nothing"! Again, there she was worrying about other people and what they would think of her. Olivia was, and still is, very fond of his parents. That was the only thing which was holding herself back from breaking free from the cage she had locked herself in! She received more messages from the Angels about her relationship; like when she would leave him, it would be the right time, she will have no worries after that, her mind will be at ease, and that she could stop carrying this baggage. Her boyfriend was like this really heavy bag of luggage, full of valuable items, and no matter how heavy and annoying this bag of luggage was, she couldn't drop it on the ground and say "I don't need you". She carried it for a whole year! He always said he loved and cared for her, I think they would have been better as friends than an item. They weren't matched personality wise; she's honest and giving, he was deep and selfish. (no offence)

Olivia has taken her relationship with him as an experience as all of us know; you can't walk over egg shells for the rest of your life, you have to make mistakes and most importantly learn by them! Olivia with her courage and the much appreciated help from the Angels, took it in her stride and ended this relationship in November 2003. She is now back to her happy self and we wouldn't have it any other way; it was tough to break it to him but she got through it and why? Because for once she was actually thinking about herself, the way she would like things and not thinking of how others would react! Typical Earth Angel right?

Always thinking of others! We have stated this experience in our book, because we wanted to give an example that Angels can help you with anything. It doesn't have to be when your dying or in trouble. They are there for even the smallest issues such as a sore finger or if you can't find a parking space; they are there to soothe your pain and help you through every single experience in your life. In other words they are your heroes; they are your rock and you can depend on them for anything! Olivia received that message one month before she ended her relationship. That is only four weeks; the Angels were her Knight in shining armours that rushed her off her feet, and rescuing her, and placing her in the highest most beautiful room in the castle, and why? because she earned to sleep in there in comfort, warmth, peace and most of all tranquillity.

Chapter 7
When The Shining Sharp blade Became A Soft Pillow.

I have always believed that Our Lord's messengers were all as one. I never would have said one Angel is more powerful than the other. They all use the same golden light, and send out positive rays to anyone in need of help, and provide a shoulder to cry on. It was only later, through my experience, that I discovered that there are different Angels that use a different light. They have a different role. They still had wings, and they still had robes, but their light was slightly different. These beings, are Archangels. Yes that's correct I said <u>Archangels</u>! You really need to pay attention! ☺ The powerful energy that rushed down through my arm when my sister Olivia had received the message about being trapped, was from an Archangel. As I have mentioned before, I sensed that they seemed higher and more powerful than the other Angels that had drawn the sketches. It was almost like they were some kind of Royalty, like God. I only learned later, that I was being visited by Archangels as well as Angels. I was very privileged! Imagine working with Angels and Archangels all at the one time. I couldn't believe it, it didn't seem reality. I have heard of many people that are inspired and touched by Angels, but I would have never known that I was one of them. Yet, little did I know I was living with an Angel (Olivia). It was almost like I was dreaming, but being fully aware; the great thing was, it had no ending, as it was information that just kept on coming.

Over the weeks after my first experience with automatic writing from the Angels, I was receiving messages everyday as well as the pictures. The written messages I received weren't very long at first. I'd just receive one or maybe two sentences, and that would be all. I don't mean to sound ungrateful, I thought to myself, but why aren't these messages getting any longer? I'm practising this for over two months now I thought, (Of course I had totally forgotten that the Angels hear every thought, every whisper). It was so brainless of me to forget about that, wouldn't you agree? Well as usual I always got my answers. The next day I had the urge to get a pencil and paper once again. It was becoming one of my daily routines, like eating breakfast or brushing your teeth. I would have a few pencils and notepads in nearly every room of house, even the bathroom! So as I was saying, the next day after I had unknowingly posted my complaint about my sentences not getting any longer (and not of any relevance or really any significance or value to my life. It was usually about Olivia's, as she is an Earth Angel. Alright!! I was feeling left out ok! I have feelings too! I thought "hey look I'm over here waving my arms in the air like a mad woman".) It wasn't that I was being selfish and wanted them to give me messages about myself. I didn't want any messages about my life, I wanted a message about what the Heavenly Dimension looked like or something related to the phenomenon! So there I was around 9.00am in the morning, with my pencil and paper again. I felt the powerful energy from the Archangels, although I hadn't received their identity yet. (As you all know there are seven Archangels: Michael, Raphael, Uriel, Chamuel, Zadkiel, Gabriel and Jophiel). I was curious to know who I was communicating with. I sensed I was receiving messages from both Archangels Raphael and Michael. I knew it had to be both, because sometimes the energy with the automatic writing would seem different. At times it would seem powerful and rushed, and at others it would feel painful as the energy was so overpowering. The pain wasn't unbearable, but my fingers and wrist would ache with pain because the energy was so powerful. After the sentence was finished, the pain would leave when the energy left. So I knew it was something to do with the power, and I wondered why do I only feel it at certain times? Then it clicked in my mind that maybe its two different Archangels! I was correct. I was receiving messages from both Archangel Raphael and Archangel Michael, but I was the one who had to differentiate between the two. I had to work out whose messages belonged to whom of the Archangels, as they had different roles. It might sound like I was getting these messages so easy, but I had little riddles to work out, and it was mentally tiring at times. Thankfully, I always succeeded with the help of Angelic Olivia and my intuitive mother Madeline.

Over the next few day's after I had complained about my very short and sweet messages from the Archangels, my message's seemed to becoming longer. They turned into three sentences, then four, and then maybe two paragraphs! My prayers were answered. I was receiving unbelievable glorious and heavenly, messages that you wouldn't read in any book! I had received a written message from the Angels saying *"You are one of our Channels for planet Earth, the world needs to know of our existence. You, and your sister Olivia are to help us generate our messages around the world. You need to heal and help those in need of comfort"*. I never seemed to feel pain down my fingers or wrist whenever I got a message which involved the words Healing or Helping , so I was beginning to recognise the difference between the two Archangels.

When I received the powerful energy, and the pain flowing down through my arm, I knew of course that it was the other Archangel, the one that seemed to have a stronger energy. So there I was, sitting at the table with this pain in my arm which was bearable yet, at the same time I wasn't really conscious of it. (Sometimes when the messages were long, I would feel like my arm was about to fall off or be brutally bruised!). Of course it never was, as the pain always left when the message was finished. The message from the painful Archangel (well, its the only way I can differentiate between the two; they aren't painful they 're very helpful actually), was.. *"I have seen the Star of David, I have cut many negative ropes in humans lives, I have fought evil, and with my sword of God I shall win!"*. Every time, when I received a message from the very powerful yet painful Archangel, he would always mention Lucifer the fallen Angel, and negative forces, but the new word he had stated which give me a clue, was the word "Sword". There is only one Angel who carries a Sword, its Archangel Michael! Now I knew that Archangel Raphael was the healer, as he always quoted about healing and helping people, and Archangel Michaels role as an Angel was, that he had to help us humans fight off negativity and evil. I hope I'm not frightening you when I use the word "evil", it doesn't mean that there is an evil man lurking behind you ready to kill you or anything. The Archangel's refer evil to bullies at school, who call you names and hurt you physically and emotionally, or people who have a low self esteem, depression, certain illnesses etc, this is what the Archangels call "an evil force at work". They are correct on that matter. This is God's world, he created it, and he would not want any of us ill or feeling down. He is full of love, he wants to help us; the reason why you feel down or ill is because of Lucifer. Yes, I am talking about Satan. I don't like his name either, but the public have to know that when your 're ill or your child's being bullied, that is not an act of God. It is Lucifer attacking innocent people, and making them feel how he would like them to feel as they are part of Gods creation. He doesn't want to destroy you personally, he wants to destroy God. He knows that when he is attacking you and making you feel worthless or sick, he is also hurting God as you are one of Gods many children and God is within each and everyone of us. The only way that you can survive if you are suffering from low self esteem (or indeed a flu!), is to be positive, and ask for Archangel Michael to cut away your negativity. Also, ask Archangel Raphael to heal and help you. You are never alone. They can and will help you. They are our Lords workers ,and they are very powerful; much more powerful than Lucifer. As he can only attack you with little things such as an infection, but he will never defeat God! As you know, in the movies, or your favourite book, Who always wins? The good or the bad? It's always the good, and it works exactly the same way on our planet. This isn't a movie however, its reality.

Archangel Raphael works with a green ray of light that helps heal and comfort those who are in need. Call on him for help and support. He will always be there, and will never let you down. Although he is invisible to the human eye, you will sense his presence. May it be feeling of heat on you, or indeed, a slight shiver up the back of your neck; that's when you know that he is there, holding your hand and protecting you. Call on Archangel Michael, to cut away your negativity with his sharp shining sword of our Lord. Again, like all the other Archangels, he will be there at your side, comforting you and fighting your demons. Archangel Michael works with a blue ray, that injects courage and stamina into you aura. You will feel stronger and more positive each day, as you pray and ask for the help from the Archangels. So if you ever catch sight of a golden hand with green beams of light shining from it, you know that its Archangel Raphael or if you see a sharp blade of a sword shining like the sun, that's Archangel Michael. That sword is your pillow. Lean your head upon it, and he will banish all your problems. If you have faith in your Angels, and have faith in God, you will survive your poverty, depression or even loss of a loved one, because your Angels are holding your hand and helping you get through your every day life. Even if you have committed a sin. Our Lord will always have a home for you in his heart. He is the creator of planet Earth and he is your father; Our Lady is your Mother and you are their children.

Chapter 8
A Light Brighter Than The sun

As we all know the sun is our warmth and energy, it regulates the climate, it helps grow our food, and it also sends out this great bright light! It is like an enormous candle that dims and flickers. Even when the sun goes down, and the sky is dark at night, the sun is still working; it shines on the moon, which acts like a mirror, reflecting light from the sun. On a hot summers day, we need our sunglasses, because the sun is so bright it makes your eyes squint. Well I've got news for you! I know of a light that is much brighter than the sun. It radiates heat like the sun, it gives light like the sun, but it is nothing like it! Try and name me a light that is so bright, yet you don't have to squint when you look at it? Take a quiet moment and think. Have you come up with anything yet? No? Well I have great privilege in knowing of a brighter light than the sun, and I am here today to inform you of it! Our world has light, so why shouldn't the Heavenly Dimension? Our Angels come with a beautiful golden light. We often wondered, How do they carry this light with them?. My first experience of seeing an Angel, was when I was doing my household chores. I heard this soothing female voice in my head, saying "Are you ready to see me?". I thought ok, at least they are warning me that they are going to appear to me. I didn't sense that this person was deceased, because the energy was coming through so powerful and I could feel a warm glow on my back. So I said "Yes I am ready to see you". I thought I was going to receive this vision through my minds eye, yet little did I know I was about to see it with my physical sight! Olivia was also in the kitchen; she had said something to me, so I glanced up at her to respond. It was then I saw these huge beautiful wings coming up from behind her. The Angel rose up behind Olivia. I then saw her face; she was very beautiful, with vivid blue eyes, and skin as white as snow, yet with a golden glow. She was wearing a blue dress, with a band of what seemed like ribbon around her waist, and she held a cross made of light. It glowed brightly in her hand. She smiled, then I blinked and she was gone. I stood there with my mouth open and staring in disbelief. I couldn't even tell Olivia that there was an Angel appearing to me from behind her. It was an overwhelming experience of joy; it had made my whole body tingle. I couldn't move, or speak. I had only came out with it when the Angel had gone. I said "Olivia I've just seen an Angel appear behind you". (Of course, I had to give a detailed description right away!) I described her every detail. From her wings to her gown; it was a miraculous sight. She had radiantly beautiful light all around her that lit up the whole room. Its an experience that everyone would enjoy, and that I will never forget. My whole body tingles with excitement when catching even a glimpse of an Angel! I later learned the name of the Angel that was drawing through me. I sensed a feminine energy every time she would send her flowing energy through my right arm. I was correct, she was a feminine force, yet I never knew her name. I always referred her to the drawing Angel or as "her", which isn't a very appropriate way to address an Angel , but I didn't know her name. It was only later that I had learned, that the Angel who appeared behind Olivia was one of her Angels, her name was Angel <u>Arielle.</u> She was the beautiful Angel I had seen, and one of the first Angels I had seen with my physical sight. I had never asked to see an Angel, as I didn't think that humans could see them with physical sight. I had asked the Angels why I had seen Arielle physically, and they informed me the next day that when your energy gets lighter, your connection to the Angels, and the Heavenly Dimension becomes stronger. We have to raise our vibration (We all have a vibrational frequency within our bodies energy field or aura) to communicate with them, and they really lower their vibration to connect with us. So in other words, as my energy was much lighter now, I was raising my frequency much higher! I was never aware that I was raising my energy higher; I didn't even know that you could do that, until the Angels told me. There have been some messages that I've received from the Angels, which are hard to understand, such as the way they inform me of Lucifer's plans to attack us humans to hurt Our Lord. I have never questioned it. I just accepted it straight away. I don't expect all you readers to do the same, I want you to question it, if you don't understand, but you will soon learn that it makes sense.

Have you ever seen a little golden glow at the side of your eye? A little flicker like a candle, when there aren't any candles around? This is not your imagination! That little glow is your guardian Angel. Even if you sense a presence with you, or feel a warm glow on your back, this is your Angel. However, not everyone has had an experience with Angels. This doesn't mean your not a good person, it can also mean that your subconscious mind would prefer not to see what you can't physically touch. There also exists the notion of worthiness. If you feel you aren't worthy of seeing your Angel, you won't; However, If you love God enough, He may deem you worthy, and you will be gifted with a glorious glimpse! Personally, I was always intrigued by the existence of Angels. I never once thought that I was going to communicate with them on a daily basis. The Spiritually Deceased also bring a light with them, very bright also, but a different energy. (I am also very grateful for the messages I receive from my deceased relatives). I love hearing from them, because there are a few I have never met, like my

Grandfather Joe. He died of a heart attack at a relatively young age; my mother didn't even get the pleasure of meeting him. Now I receive regular visits from him.

My first visit from my Grandfather Brady, was when I was reading Olivia's cards. I had given her the cards to shuffle (To be able to read someone's cards, they have to place their energy into them; thus the shuffle). As she chose seven cards out of the thirty six deck, I turned them over as she handed them to me. I gave her some information about her life; that she was going to receive more clients this week, and that she would receive some news from a man that she already knew. She couldn't think of who that would be, but time would tell as the seven spread displays your week ahead. I also received that she would have a spiritual experience. During the reading, I sensed a male energy in the room. I didn't speak of this to her, until I read the rest of her cards. (I always ask spirits if they don't mind waiting before they give me information on their identity, and their message if any if I have already started a reading, as it simplifies the process for me, and the person I am reading for). When I had finished reading her cards, I told her of the male presence I had sensed in the room. I then asked the spirit who was trying to deliver a message, to tell me a little about himself. I received an image of a donkey, a fiddle, and a little terrier dog. The only person I knew of who played the fiddle, was my Grandfather Brady. That was the main thing that I knew about him, and of course, the way he died. I asked if he was Grandfather Brady and I received a strong yes. As usual, I always doubted myself, so I asked for another image to reinforce my gut feeling. I had thought about my father at work, and what he was doing. I received an image of a grey door. I didn't question him for anymore information. He then said he was here, because he wanted to tell Olivia that he is one of her spirit guides. He chose to guide her life, as she was the oldest girl in our family. Olivia was really pleased with this information; he also said that he had a soft spot for her, because she played the fiddle. My Grandfather was a great fan of Irish traditional music. It has carried on through our family, thanks to our parents. Suddenly I sensed his energy drifting away, and I couldn't connect with him anymore. He had just come to introduce himself to Olivia. Now that he had a way of connecting to us, through me, he thought he'd let her know that he is one of her guides. When my father came home from work that evening, I thought I'd mention the grey door that Grandfather Brady had told me about. He said that where he was working that day there was a mobile canteen that he and the work men had ate their lunch in that had a grey door. I was pleased that I had heard my Grandfathers thoughts correctly, and told him that he had visited when I was reading Olivia's cards. The other details during the reading also checked out with him. Olivia received more clients that week. She also received a phone call from her ex boyfriend; everything I had predicted came true! They may only be trivial things that my Grandfather shared with me, but they meant something to my father; it showed that he was watching over him everyday, and that just because he was gone physically, it didn't mean that he was gone forever.

One afternoon, I was sitting in Olivia's holistic healing room, doing a spread of Angel cards that my mother had bought for me. As I put the cards back into their box, I felt like there was someone watching me. Have you ever had that feeling, where you feel someone is behind you ? Well when you experience that, your probably correct. My mother then came into the room and she sat down. She did a spread of the Angel cards for herself.(You don't really need someone to read them for you, as there are messages displayed on each card.) As I was sitting there, I saw in my minds eye, my mothers father and her sister Eileen with a really white bright light surrounding them both. It was such a massive thing to see; they were almost like the size of toddlers, standing in front of it. It reminded me of a sunset only it was really bright. I didn't have to squint; it wasn't sore on my eyes. It was outstanding!. My Grandfather and my aunt Eileen, started to walk back into this light. They didn't seem to be there to give me a message. I questioned why they didn't speak. I was wrong to question however, as they gave me a message. They had displayed it to me; the light they were surrounded by! They were showing me that there is a light much brighter than the sun. It doesn't hurt the physical eye, there is no need to squint, you can use your full vision. I was bowled over that I was able to receive such a beautiful sight. The sun (and moon) may shine bright on our lives, but you will never see such light as the white light of heaven until your Soul has been fulfilled, and you are invited into Heaven. (You'll find the colours of your 'Bodysuit' aren't as bright as they once were when first received it. It has faded, and there may even be a few holes! Don't worry though, God will let you know when this trade needs to happen). So you are then ready to trade in your old suit for a new one. You leave the planets light behind, and cross over the bridge, to greet a new light, that will be much brighter than the sun. ☺

Chapter 9
If Water Can Run
Freely, So Can You

Our lives run like the water in a river. We get over the problems and blockages in our lives, in exactly the same way as a rivers water can seep through or creep over big rocks and stones on its way to the sea. Your probably thinking, how you can relate your life to this. Its simple really. Some people have lives of ease and luxury; others, have much more difficulty. Everyone in our world have their problems though. If your having a bad hair day, what do you do? You either make an appointment with a hairdresser, or sort it out yourself. That's the positive outcome in that instance, (you've gotten over that little blockage!) However, people can have much larger blockages to their happiness, such as suffering from a terminal illness, or dealing with all the issues within broken homes or relationships. Human nature can make us very resilient; either way, we *can* all get through it. We encounter the rock in our stream, and no matter how big it is, if we stay positive, and say I am going to get over that, it doesn't matter how long it takes, we will see what's on the other side!! In these cases, a highly positive attitude is the key. Some situations make it difficult to think positively. To much concentration and thought on the negative, will bring you down. You will suffer a definite drop in self esteem, and in the worst instance, from depression. Do something that makes you feel good. Go shopping, visit a friend, talk your problems over, never keep them in because that will create a blockage in your life. The longer you hold a problem in, the bigger it will get. I have a friend who was bullied all her life. She hated school, hated her appearance, and most of all hated everybody in her class. They tortured her mind all the time. There was name calling, comments about her being overweight, her hair, everything about her physical body that you can think of. Imagine waking up every morning and not wanting to live?, all because of the selfish immature students of both sexes in her class. They didn't care about her feelings, or if she had a wonderful personality. They looked at her as someone who was quiet, in other words, a perfect target. I was her good friend. I kept her positive. I made her laugh. I stood by her and defended her. I know that my giving her support and that little bit of positivity, stopped her from being six feet under. Her family knew nothing of the way she was treated in school, until one day I told her mother. She spoke to her class teacher, who reprimanded the culprits severely, especially the ones that needed it. It stopped for a while, but then it began again, right up until she left High school basically. I was still the same friend as I always was to her, and she took comfort in that, to help her through what was an extended period of unhappiness for her. And now? She is a healthy and beautiful person, inside and out. She has lost all her weight, and has a great job. (Unfortunately, it's only now that people can see her perfect personality!). Her beauty is shining brighter than ever. I have shared this story with you because that was a blockage in her life and it was torture, but guess what? She got over that huge rock and she seen the sun shining bright at the other side. Her strength of character and determination helped her to see the positivity in each and every bad situation she faced. She realised life is worth living and she enjoys it to the full!

If you have a blockage in your life, a reliance on God will always remove it for you. Personally, as a Catholic, I say the rosary every night, and ask for Our Lord and Our Lady's help. The rosary is a very powerful prayer. It's a protection for anyone who says it with thought. I always receive an answer to the question I have asked God. However, I know that not all the readers of this book are Catholic like myself and Olivia. We are trying to bring to your mind the concept of Gods complete love for everyone, and His promise of help to all who ask. So whoever, or whatever you believe God to be, take the time to ask, when a problem or blockage arrives into your life. You will find that if you are in need, and look deep into your soul to ask for help........ God *will* answer you.

A very common cause of blockages or deep rooted problems in very many peoples lives, lies within the realms of relationships. When your heart is broken because your partner has left you, or broken because you can't find love, major problems will occur. Don't worry. There is a soul mate for everyone out there. If you have not met yours yet, you will. God would not want any of his children to die lonely without exchanging vows with someone they love. To this end, He created an Archangel to look over emotional issues. Her name is Archangel Chamuel. Pray to her. She won't hesitate to help you. She works with a pink ray which comforts your emotional side of the body, so if your seeking help from God, pray to both him and Archangel Chamuel. Also St Valentine can help you. (Yes, He is real. Its not just about roses and chocolates!!) Those of you that don't know St Valentines background, I will explain. St Valentine was a priest many years ago, that married in secret, those who where already married, or didn't have permission from their parents. He only broke his law as a priest, because he seen that the couples he married were in love. As he once stated, "To love is not to be selfish". So in a way, he helped those who had blockages within relationships. He can help you too. Affection, or lack of it, can be one of the biggest blockages in a huge amount of people lives. Olivia once had a client, who was married to a very wealthy man. He bought her everything, she lead a luxurious life, classy car, mansion of a house, expensive holidays,….. sounds perfect doesn't it? Well it wasn't. Her husband didn't show her much affection at all. She was like an ornament that he would carry around with him and set where he wanted it to be placed. She was suicidal and suffered from Anorexia as a result. You would think that your husband would notice that your depressed, and losing loads of weight wouldn't you? He didn't. He thought she would be that bit more perfect if she styled her hair differently, bought new clothes, and, believe it or not, *lost that little bit more weight!* She was a beautiful woman the way she was. Of course he didn't see that. It wasn't love on his side, or even hers. She had met him when she was very young, and since her father died when she was at a very young age, she was searching for more of a father figure than a lover. He was ten years her senior. He didn't care if she had a brain, as long as she kept herself looking young and beautiful. That's all that mattered to him. He didn't want to listen; he was the one that did the talking, she was the one that did the listening. If you are living with a partner who is similar to this person, get out. Save yourself. A person like that, be they male or female, will not change. They don't believe they are wrong, therefore, they will not take up the challenge of this change. Don't be afraid that you won't ever meet anyone else; the same woman I am talking about, left her selfish unloving husband, (which took a lot of courage) and now she has the strength of a lion. (not physically of course, only Samson was blessed with that!). The Catholic Religion believe that marriage should be for life. However, in some situations an annulment should be granted. If you are living with someone who doesn't treat you in the way you deserve, you're best to leave, and start your life over again with someone else. In other words, take a brand new clean page and dispose of your old crinkly torn piece of paper.

Now do you understand when I relate our lives to water? We all have rocks and stones to climb over. Sometimes these rocks can be as big as a mountain, but if water can get over it, or through it, why can't we? Don't hide behind the rock because you are afraid that you won't be able to get over it. You will. Look at the two stories I have shared with you. They are very real. If they can escape big situations like that, so can you! So think of yourself as water. You can run or trickle over that rock; you choose the pace you will take. Time is a healer, but don't leave it too long! There is a beautiful rainbow at the other side of that rock. The sun shines bright; the grass might not be any greener, but at least you will be free from stress. You won't be suffocating any longer. You will be able to breath , but most of all LIVE!!

Chapter 10
Deceased People Also
Can Guide Your Life,
As Well As Angels

When we die, what do we do? Sit around all day under a tree, maybe reading a book on a beautiful sunny day? WRONG! When your loved ones pass over, they are kept busy. Just because they aren't here physically in our world, does not mean that they don't have a role in the next! As the wonderful Archangels and Angels have informed me, our world is just an illusion. It may seem real, but when you pass over, you will soon learn, that when you look back on your old world, it certainly won't be reality! Picture a little goldfish swimming around its small bowl. It doesn't know of the existence of any other world; only the confined space it lives in. It works exactly the same in the Heavenly Dimension. We are the goldfish in the bowl, and they look in on us; watching us, and guiding us. Almost everyone in our world has lost a loved one. My mother lost her sister tragically. I have mentioned her name before, (Eileen) although I have never explained to you how she died. Eileen died in 1986, at just seventeen years of age. Her whole life was in front of her. Why would God take such a young life?, you may ask. This occurs all over the world all the time. You can only imagine the grief that any family would suffer; our hearts go out to you all. Eileen had a boyfriend and was thinking of starting a hair dressing course. She was very funny and full of life, (she couldn't sit down for any length of time, in other word's she had ants in her pants!) Your probably curious that at just the age of twenty, I sound like I knew her personally; I was only two years old when she passed over to the Heavenly Dimension. As I have mentioned before, I have a great memory; its almost like a computer. I store the good, the bad, and even the ugly, under some file in my mind,(I am not a robot I assure you). My earliest memory of my aunt Eileen, was in my Grandparents old house. I was only about eighteen months old; it was my aunts birthday. I was sitting on my mothers lap when my mother handed me a present to give to her. I remember running really fast to her, throwing it at her, and then running as fast as I could back to mum. Everyone laughed at this speedy child, (which was me!). Eileen was sitting on the window sill, looking at this, and laughing also. She was wearing white jeans and a yellow short sleeved top; this is my only memory of her. Eileen was knocked down by a car, as she was walking with her boyfriend. They were crossing a bridge walking hand in hand, when the car hit her. It knocked her over the bridge and into the water; she hit her head on the way down and was unconscious as she hit the water. She was slowly drowning. The ambulance came and the paramedic tried to revive her. He asked that if she could hear him, to stick out her tongue. She did. The family then thought great, she might get through this ok. Their hearts were to be torn however, as they watched their little baby sister, the youngest in their home, make no further movement hooked up to a life support machine. The only movement Eileen made, was the night before she died around 6.00am. Eileen had closed her arms over. My mother and my aunt Carmel were present. They were told that it was a very rare muscular spasm, which caused the movement of the limbs. At around that same time back home in my Grandparents house, my Grandmother heard Eileen calling out to her "mummy". Eileen was saying goodbye to her mother, as it would be the last time my Grandmother would ever physically hear her.

Wouldn't it be very sad to think that at such a young age, Eileen would be buried and that would be the end of her? Its an outlook that has sadly become all to familiar nowadays; namely that death is the end. I pity anyone who has that outlook on death, because life goes on after it. (A life that is much better than ours here on Earth, I might add!). I have had many visits from my godmother Eileen. She has warned me about things, and has laughed with my family and I. She isn't dead. She is living out her life in the Heavenly Dimension. It has been eighteen years since she has passed; she is still wearing the same clothes that she wore in her time as a teenager, and most of all, she still has that outstanding wonderful personality she had when she was with us. In other words, she still has ants in her pants!

My Grandfather Coney (who is my mother's father), suffered from cancer at the age of forty nine. He had part of his lung removed, but was never told he had cancer. It was felt by his doctor, that knowledge of his illness would have taken his pride and dignity to a large degree. My Grandfather was a very tall handsome man, and had a reputation as being very quiet. He was very hardworking; he worked cutting turf. One Sunday he was working, when he started to see vivid colours swirling around on the ground. He then looked up and he saw the Child Of Prague before him. He never quite new why the Child Of Prague appeared before him, he thought it was because he was working on a Sunday. I am sure he has gotten his answer now though, as he is in the Heavenly Dimension. (An explanation of The Child of Prague will be given at the end of the book, for those who don't know the tale.)

Although he was diagnosed with cancer at the age of forty nine, he didn't pass over until the year 2000. He was eighty-two. He had fought off this disease for all those years.

The year he died, he was diagnosed with lung cancer. This was the first time his family knew of his body suffering from the disease all those years ago. My Grandfather has visited me a few times, since I discovered my gift to connect with the deceased. He is very powerful in the Heavenly Dimension, and so is my Godmother Eileen. They are completely surrounded by a bright golden light. They guide and look after all of our family. My Grandfather was a very religious man, and after him sharing his story of the Child of Prague appearing to him, each of us have a statue of the Child of Prague in our home. When I see the Child of Prague statue anywhere, I instantly think of my Grandfather, the tall handsome quiet man. My only living Grandparent, Lucy Coney. She has a great spirit, and although she is seventy seven, she is the one with the youngest heart out of us all. We love you Granny; you make us laugh until our stomachs hurt. The Grandparent that I have not yet introduced to you, is my Grandmother Agnes Brady, my fathers mother. My only memories of my Grandmother, are of her walking around outside wearing her pink and navy apron, feeding the kittens, goats and hens. Another memory of her is when she became ill, and took a stroke, losing the use of her left side. This little country woman, who loved walking around outside and looking after her small farm, had to endure being confined to a bed or her chair. She died on December 29th 1993, at the age of seventy nine. Strangely enough, her husband, my Grandfather Joe Brady, died on exactly the same date, December 29th although he died much earlier, in 1976, aged sixty. Our loved ones that have passed and left us behind to grieve, do not blame or get angry with Our Lord. They are in a much more positive world. They are extremely happy, and watch over and guide you through your lives. Angels guide, and so do your deceased loved ones. Just because they don't have wings, doesn't mean they aren't experienced enough to guide your life. They have a wealth of experience, as they once lived here on Earth as well. My brother Stephen and his wife Anita, will be married a year in June. They live in my Grandparent Brady's old home. One night when I was visiting them, Anita asked me to read her cards. Anita is a very open minded person and very down to Earth. As I was reading her cards, I sensed that my Grandmother Brady was present. I asked her to give me an image, or tell me of something that had happened recently in the house that I wouldn't know of. I instantly heard a loud banging noise in my head like as if something had fallen off a wall and smashed. It didn't seem like a plate; it sounded wooden. I asked Anita if anything had fallen off any of her walls. Anita told me that the day before, a wooden sculpture she had received as a wedding present, had fallen and smashed outside the bedroom where my Grandparents had slept. It turns out, that my Grandmother Brady had been admiring it, and had accidentally knocked it down. She came in simply to give Anita her sincere apologies for knocking down her wedding gift. Anita sat in amazement. She accepted her apology. It was enough evidence for her that there is life after death. On one other occasion when I was doing a card reading for Anita, I seen that she would happen to find money somewhere, maybe inside an envelope or something. I also sensed a woman present, although it was a different energy. I knew it wasn't any of my family, so I asked her to give me her first initial. I was receiving an M sound, like Maureen or Mary. I said these names, and she said that she had an aunt Mary who had died of breast cancer. I then asked Mary to send me something that Anita had done recently that I wouldn't know. I then got the scent of sea air. I asked her about this. Anita's mouth dropped open. She said she had only returned home from the beach with her mother and sister. I then felt the energy drifting away; her aunt was visiting, to tell Anita that she guides and watches over her life, just as my Grandfather Brady watches over Olivia's. A few days later, she was clearing out her spare room. Anita came across a wedding card with money inside! I had predicted that she would find money, and she did!

These may seem trivial things, but you cannot discount their significance. It takes considerable effort for your deceased loved ones to make contact with you, to let you know that they are watching over and guiding you. It is a wonderful experience. If you *have* lost a loved one, you will grieve. You may suffer this grief for years, but please remember, those that have passed would not want this. However, they will also help you through that process. When you shed your tears for the loss of loved one, the person who has died, is sitting beside you, catching each and everyone of your tear drops. Try to sense their presence, and you will soon realise, that they may be gone physically, but they still love you, and are there, with your Angels, to help and guide you until you meet again.

Chapter 11
Medication: Not
always the answer!

Do you, or anyone you know, hear voices in their head? The first reaction from 99% of people in this position is to assume that they're crazy. Right? Wrong! Most people who receive medication to block out these voices are not suffering from a mental illness. We have a relative, who was diagnosed as schizophrenic, from he was an adolescent. He is now a grown man of forty seven. The tragedy is, it is only now that we have discovered that he was actually a highly gifted child of Our Lord. Of course when he was diagnosed, society was vastly different than it is now. There weren't as many psychics or mediums around, and if there were, they kept it secret, as they would have been viewed as crazy. We have changed his name throughout this chapter to protect his privacy, so we have decided to call him "Patrick". From Patrick was a child, he heard many voices, not mentally but physically. His name was called often, and yet there was no one there to physically respond to. Patrick was a man of prophecy. He predicted many happenings, even the tragic events of September 11th, in 2001. I remember a time when we visited him. I was only a child around seven; my interest in the adults conversation was very limited, but I do remember Patrick telling my mother and I that scientists would invent a computer that connect people all over the world. Of course e-mail and the World Wide Web are as common-place as the telephone nowadays, but its very interesting that he thought of it when he did. That is only one of his predictions! Patrick has had checks in and out of a local mental institution whenever he felt he wasn't well. He felt more secure there during these times, and would always admit himself in. Our family have full faith in Patrick. We know that he is not mentally ill; the voices he has heard, have been the Spiritually Deceased. He has seen Our Lady and even Lucifer. Our Lady appeared to Patrick to give him strength, and to ask him to pray to her whenever he wasn't well. When you have a connection with the other realms, you can attract energies that are both negative and positive. This has nothing to do with you as a person. As the Angels have explained, when your able to connect to the Heavenly Realm, you shine like a light in a dark room, (in other words we can be spotted a mile away!). This is what has happened to Patrick. His light shone bright, the deceased saw it, and tried to connect with him. They needed his help; that is why they called upon him. Patrick was, and still is, a very religious man. His room is decorated with beautiful religious statues and rosary beads. This is his protection from negativity creeping in; his faith in his religion keeps him strong. It is a great pity that Patrick did not know of any psychics or Spiritualist Mediums at the time, as he wouldn't have gone down the path of institutions, or of having his state of mind questioned. He certainly wouldn't have been put on a strong medication for the rest of his life; he cannot be cured now, as the medication over the years has damaged his whole nervous system. Patrick has spoken to the Archangels and Angels. He has a letter from Archangel Raphael, that had to be placed under his pillow, to calm his mind. The Angels also sketched Patrick a drawing of his Angel of light, which he keeps in a frame in his room. Since he has received his Angel of light, he has been much more level mentally. As you may know, many schizophrenics suffer from mood swings and can be violent at times, but not Patrick. The reason for this, is that he doesn't suffer from a mental illness. He is a caring, loving and giving person. Its a pity that he is only learning now he is a blessed child of Our Lords. If you know of any one that suffers from a mental illness, or even if you are on medication for a mental illness and have experienced many happenings like Patrick, remember that the voices you hear may just be the real thing! The Angels will help you in every way they can, to firstly, help you realise that you may have a gift from God, and secondly, to help you develop your gift, and give you the strength and courage to confront any trials you may face because of it. Ask for Archangel Michael, to cut away all negativity with his sword of Our Lord, and Archangel Raphael to heal your mental and emotional wounds. However, belief in yourself is of the utmost importance, (with a healthy dose of humility of course!) To say that your normal like everyone else, isn't exactly true though. Sure we socialise like any other people, but we have that little sparkle in our eye that says we know a lot more than we are telling. We are gifted and most of all we are blessed! So, if you feel you are `special` in that way, don't despair! You are not alone, nor are you anything to be *ridiculed*!

We have read many books on the subject of Angels, and have found a lack of information about the negative side to it all. Certainly, Our Lords Angels, dwell in the realms of light, and give their full attention to the service of God, and the guidance of humanity. However, there is something that a lot of publications leave out.......Lucifer exists. He exists, and hell exists, just as Our Lord and Heaven exist. His sole purpose is to destroy all that God wants to achieve, and he will use all the methods he can. One such method, is the use of voices in your head, to influence the physical body. A good way to differentiate between good and bad influence is this. Lucifer will try to send you down a pathway of wrong, in your actions and thought; Our Lords Angels *will only guide you for your highest good, and toward Heaven.* Our Lord has a constant battle to fight with Lucifer the fallen Angel. Our lord would not say he is at war; Lucifer wants war, that is why he influences all of us here on Earth without us realising it. Drugs, Alcohol, and Sex, are abused and misused everywhere, and at all times. Also, judging, vicious gossip and ridicule are rife in every society, and we can all fall into those particular categories at times! Our Lord's ways might seem that they aren't easy to follow and that Lucifer's are. However what a lot of people don't see, is that Lucifer is destroying you, where as Our Lord wants to save you! Drug and alcohol abuse can be so easy to do nowadays; its not hard to get either any more (such are Lucifer's attempts to ruin all the good we have to offer as Gods children). These destroy your physical body, and ruin your mind; both of which Our Lord has given you to look after, your body is your temple you must keep all pathway's clear! All Our Lord asks of us is to put war aside, give out positive energy, pray, and have faith in Him and His workers. Our Lord is quite clear on this also; do not judge or ridicule, as you are listening to Lucifer when you are doing this. What Our Lord asks of us is easy. Did Lucifer die on a cross for his people? No he did not! Do not worship him. Worship the true creator of the universe; the Man that would forgive you for your sins. Lucifer makes you carry out your sins. Our Lord has suffered enough for us, we should not add to this. As you can tell we feel very strongly about this subject, just as other people with Angel connections and spiritual gifts from God, always ignoring Lucifer and his empty promises. This leaves our work more difficult, when so much misinformation is out there. So, in conclusion, these gifts can arrive in various ways, one of which is a voice, or voices in your head. We have stated that so many people think they are mentally sick, or incapable, and so they renounce their gifts from God. All we advise you is to seek help with this first, investigating the possibility of a divine source for the phenomenon. It won't hurt to try. You never know, what starts out as something that shocks you, could end up being a source of help and inspiration to many others.

Chapter 12
A Spiritual Butterfly,
Each Flutter Is Real

We all know what butterflies look like; their beautiful colours, their gentle manner, the way their wings flutter! There is a lot more to butterflies than you think!. Each creature of Our Lords have spirituality from insects to mammals. Take dolphins for instance. They are very gentle creatures, they communicate and can even cure us humans! Butterflies work much in the same way. We are all part of the one Creation. The Angels have told me that butterflies have a very spiritual significance; they care and can even heal us humans. They are part of the Angel Dimension, Heaven sent, yet living here on Earth. A majority of butterflies are just normal, its the yellow ones you must look out for! An Angel can be disguised as a butterfly; think about it, Angels have wings and so do butterflies, it is only common sense that they will come in a form of a creature that has wings. You might think why not a bird? Well, they can come in a form of bird, such as a dove. This starts a certain debate within the realms of `Angel work`. I have read many books about people who have a connection with the Heavenly Realm. They see they're Angels with feathered wings. Throughout the months since I have discovered my gift, any Angels that have appeared to me have wings, but they are not feathered. They are made of golden light. This sparked my interest greatly, and I asked the Angels why others have seen them with feathered wings. One of my Angels told me, that if their companion on Earth, whom they have guided from birth, imagines Angels to have feathered wings, the Angels then appear to them with feathered wings. Its a way for the

Angels to appear, that won't cause anyone fear. Personally, I have never pictured Angels with feathered wings. I don't know why; I just thought the idea of an Angel with feathered wings was weird, and yet I have always pictured Archangel Michael with feathered wings. However, the images of any other Archangel or Angel with feathered wings, didn't seem right in my opinion. (This is why my Angels appear to me with non feathered wings) Angels are Angels, they can appear to us in many different forms, even as a human.

I have a cousin who once was a very heavy smoker; he was only 20 and he was smoking twenty five to thirty cigarettes a day! That is a lot of cigarettes for a young person to inhale in one day, especially when he wasn't even under much stress. Sure, he was at university, but he had just started smoking socially about three months before his addiction. It then formed into an every day thing; he was no longer just smoking socially! I have decided to name him Emmett. Once Emmett had heard that Olivia and I had a connection with Angels, he was the first on the phone, "Hey, is it true you have a connection with Angels?" I was totally taken back that he knew. I was also worried about what he would think! Its not every day you get to explain to people that you have a connection with Angels and that they would totally understand. I am the kind of person that always worries about what other people will think, they could maybe say that I was crazy Olivia was overjoyed that he knew! (She thought great, why shouldn't people know of our connection to our Angels, it's a privilege to have the connection in the first place!). Olivia's outlook was entirely appropriate.

She didn't care what anyone thought, she thought "People either except it or they don't, no big deal". Emmett made an appointment with Olivia for a treatment, as she does I.E.T (Integrated Energy Therapy). He also wanted to ask who his

Angels were, and if they had a message for him. At first I wasn't comfortable explaining everything to Emmett about our connection with the Angels. I basically found it hard to explain; there I was with this blessed gift and yet I couldn't put into words what it all meant! I told Emmett about the Angels being able to write through me and draw. Although he listened, something was telling me that he was a little sceptical; which is understandable (even though I hated the fact of him being like that, but I know I have to accept that, in this line of work). Emmett had questioned the Angels all about Our Lord. He had asked questions about Jesus and the Ten Commandments; at first I thought Emmett was testing the Angels, as he knew I wouldn't have known a lot about the Bible. I think he was shocked when he left though, as the Angels answered each and every one of his questions to perfection! (Of course!) Emmett knows that I wasn't at all pleased when he questioned the Angels, but now he has a different outlook, don't you Emmett? (He better say yes). Emmett came up at weekends to learn more about his Angels. One of the questions that Emmett asked the Angels was their thoughts on cigarettes and other drugs. Archangel Raphael was answering Emmett's questions that evening. He is Our Lords Angel concerning health matters (Amongst many other things of course!) He stated that Lucifer helped in the creation of cigarettes, as they destroy the physical body, which was created by God. Archangel Raphael said that when you inhale cigarettes or take drugs, you sit with the fallen Angel Lucifer! If you are a smoker do not be alarmed, he isn't going to kill you off or anything, your already doing that yourself in the first place by inhaling nicotine! That may seem harsh, but take a look at what ingredients are in cigarettes; rat poison, tar, toilet cleaner and even nail varnish remover! (Yes you heard me, even nail varnish remover!) As Archangel Raphael was explaining all the dangers to Emmett of cigarettes and other drugs, Emmett took a moment of quiet thought and said "I've decided I want to quit, how can you help me Raphael?" Archangel Raphael then wrote on the page, that he would insert a beautiful golden butterfly from the Heavenly Dimension into his lungs. Each time the butterfly would flutter its wings, positive energy rays would radiate from them, thus helping the process and almost satisfying the craving for the nicotine! You might be thinking, what good is this butterfly going to do in the first place? Again I have an answer, thanks to my Angels! The main issue of receiving the butterfly is that you cannot harm it. Archangel Raphael was allowing Emmett only fifteen cigarettes to smoke every day; if he went over that amount, the butterfly would suffocate in his lungs, with the overdose of nicotine! To all you animal lovers out there, do not be alarmed. If the butterfly was to die in the persons lung, Archangel Raphael would retrieve it from there and revive it, placing it back in the Heavenly Dimension again. Of course you can only receive this grace once, as it would be unfair to put another butterfly through the same experience as the last one! Archangel Raphael gave Emmett a sketch of his beautiful butterfly. He was also asked to promise not to harm it, by going over the fifteen a day. Archangel Raphael sent a golden ray of light to Emmett, placing the butterfly into his lungs, and told him that he would be cutting down his cigarettes to only twelve a day in two weeks. Emmett accepted this; he found it hard the first week, but he did much better the second. (And all because of the butterfly radiating off positive rays each time it fluttered; he probably would have had an attitude of failure instead of flutter!) Emmett then came back after two weeks to see if he could get them cut down again. Archangel Raphael, put him on a minimum of twelve cigarettes a day; to return again in two weeks. Emmett was doing fine with just being able to have this amount, until one day he was working and lost count. Emmett rang me in complete panic thinking he had killed his butterfly. I asked Archangel Raphael if Emmett had destroyed this beautiful creature; thankfully he didn't, although the butterfly's light wasn't as bright and it was lacking oxygen. Archangel Raphael then informed me that for Emmett to revive his butterfly, he must not smoke for at least twelve hours. He was grateful to hear that his butterfly was still alive as he couldn't of kept it on his conscience if he had killed it. Emmett carried out this task, and his butterfly's light became brighter. This carried on for many of weeks; Archangel Raphael healed and helped his lungs by cutting his addiction gradually down. He allowed Emmett a minimum of cigarettes to smoke, it went down to seven, then five, and then three; three months down the line from he first began his task to fight his addiction, he became a non smoker! He has not smoked at all ever since! Archangel Raphael saved his young lungs, and now he can run, swim, and most of all inhale fresh air like he never could before. His butterfly is still with him, radiating positive rays and keeping him optimistic!

My mother was also a smoker. Archangel Raphael who is her Guardian Angel, saved her also. He gave her a butterfly also, and she has never smoked since. Archangel Raphael kept her strong, (with the help of her little Heavenly friend!) so if your ever thinking of killing off your addiction, forget about nicotine patches, and gum. Here are two people that have tried these methods to help them with their addiction; the only one that worked was a Heavenly butterfly! If you suffer from any addiction, it consumes your life, be it as simple as a cigarette, or as life altering, as a drug or gambling problem. The Angels are waiting to help as soon as you ask! Ask them to simply place a butterfly into the area affected (Your lungs for smoking, your stomach for alcohol, your mind for gambling etc..), give God control over your life, and follow your guidance. It would also be a good idea to let someone know that you have begun to do this, as support from a friend or family member will always help you through.(Of course the Angels will be assisting them also. It's a win win situation!!) You will find that you will not want to harm this beautiful Heaven sent creature, as it is alive in your body. It will be your responsibility though; you must keep it safe, shelter it well and most of all protect it! However there has been a few unfortunate clients that didn't quite succeed with their little fluttering friend, because of their weakness in faith in the man above. But fortunate for those who did fail did get another healing in a different area of their lives. Be strong. Thankfully most of my clients that have accepted this fluttering challenge has conquered their addiction,. A BIG CONGRATULATIONS to all of you! (you know who you are). If you choose a pathway that leaves you with a troublesome addiction, the Angels through their little fluttering friend, will give you the courage to succeed. If my mother and Emmett can do it, so can you. They can be your inspiration, whatever addiction you face.

Chapter 13
What Do The Angels
Actually Do?

Angels were Our Lords creation before us humans. Our Lord created the Angels to help His creations on Earth, (such as all animals and mankind). He needed messengers to help Him rule and keep our planet safe; this is why each and every one of us, whether good or bad have a guardian Angel from birth. One evening, I was sitting thinking about what Angels actually are. I thought, I have this connection with the Heavenly Dimension, and I have never actually asked them what they are or what their Dimension is actually like. I knew Angels were messengers for Our Lord; everyone knows that. I wanted more detail, I needed to know if they slept, ate, or if they had bodies like us. The next day I received my answer. Once again, the Angels heard my most private inner thoughts.! Archangel Raphael came to satisfy my curiosity. He stated that Angels are all as one, we humans, their companions on Earth, create their identity. We choose whether our guardian Angels are male or female. As humans, we have both a masculine and feminine side. Our Angels `gender`, if you like, will depend upon the male/female balance within your body. If you are a male that is more in touch with your feminine side, you will have more `female` Angels, and vice versa. Most of us however, have a healthy balance in this regard, and therefore, we would tend to have Angels of both genders. Archangel Raphael also stated that Angels cannot see with the physical eye like we can, they only see our souls. This does not mean that the Angels are blind. Of course not!. They `see` our souls as being made up of all the colours of the rainbow, and more; much the same as

72

you would have seen in a glass prism in High School, right? They can see physically in the Heavenly Dimension but not in ours. (When the Angels refer us to being Earth bound, this means that our dimension, planet Earth and our galaxy etc, is the lowest dimension from the Heavenly. In other words, we are just tagging along, we Earthlings are last in line in the dimension pathway!) Archangel Raphael informed me that, when they communicate with any of us humans here on Earth, they have to lower their vibrations to do so, whereas we humans have to raise our vibrations to connect with their Heavenly Dimension. It's almost like the Angels have to take an elevator and press one Dimension down to connect to us, where as we would have to press one Dimension up! Well that's how the Angels see, and how they communicate with us! I also learned that Angels cannot hear like us humans. Don't fret! Your prayers are not being ignored! The Angels can't hear us in the conventional way, they read our thoughts. Archangel Raphael explained to me, that they can read our thoughts just like we would read a novel or the newspaper. They don't however, have a miniature typewriter, typing our every word down; each thought we think, our Guardian Angels hear by thought. Archangel Raphael has heard of my mothers thoughts as he is her guardian Angel. When my mother heard this she laughed, and said "Tell me one of my thoughts today Raphael?" He then wrote her an answer. I read aloud "You were thinking that you would love to write like us Angels just an Earth time second ago" My mother was almost swept off her feet with shock! As she was waiting for Archangel Raphael's reply, she had been thinking at that exact moment, that she admired the Angels handwriting. Archangel Raphael had instantly heard the thought, like we would hear someone on the other end of the telephone! I don't however, want you all to suffer from paranoia, now that you know your Angels can read your every thought! We are human. We might have some bad thoughts about this and that, but our Angels are there listening to help and guide us; they do not judge our lives, Our Lord does! (That's even more terrifying isn't it?) Archangel Raphael also informed me, that Angels do not have physical bodies like us, they are simply made up of golden energy from Our Lord. They have partners, but not like the partners we have here on Earth. Our Angels partners are like business partners; they are always of the opposite sex and they help each other guide and heal us down here on Earth.

Angels all have different roles. Archangel Raphael's role for example is to heal. He principally deals with humanity in this capacity; he has not experienced laughter or sadness in the conventional sense, as he is not an Angel of emotion. Although Archangel Raphael has stated that he can relate to all of the humans on Earths problems as he reads their energy, feeling and knowing every emotion at that present time, whatever the situation. We even have Angels of duty, that will help us get us a parking space. (Try this one out. Even if you have lasted this long in the book, and you are a certified sceptic......it does work, every time!) Any duty at all, even if you have lost something, ask your Angel of duty to help you find it, and it will suddenly appear out of nowhere! I sat thinking about what Archangel Raphael had written about Angels, not being able to laugh or experience sadness. I thought that was a little strange, as they help people with their problems. I couldn't imagine the Angels not being able to experience what their companions on Earth were. Archangel Raphael stated, that if you were in a state of depression for example, you have an Angel of positivity to help you; they will send you rays of golden energy to make you feel more positive. Even if you are a selfish person, you will have an Angel to help guide you to be more giving. The Angel would send you golden giving rays from the Heavenly Dimension. Archangel Raphael also explained to me about the Heavenly Dimension. He said that there are birds, trees, sunlight, water falls, animals, insects, warmth and most of all love. The Heavenly Dimension is full of love; all beings there communicate by thought, they are at peace, and have complete tranquillity. Archangel Raphael gave me a miraculous vision of a certain part of the Heavenly Dimension. I was meditating in the healing room in our house, with my focus upon the Angelic Realm, when to my amazement, I was standing in a very peaceful atmosphere, in the most beautiful garden. All the colours seemed so vivid, the sounds were so clear to me; I knew I wasn't dreaming! There were butterfly's, and an amazing array of all kinds of birds singing in the cloudless sky, ; the light was outstanding, completely white; I could feel it warm on my skin. There wasn't a cloud in the sky, the grass was a healthy green and the trees swayed in the light breeze. It was perfect. It was Heavenly. Suddenly I felt like I was being sucked up by a vacuum and spat out into my home again. I hadn't experienced anything like that before. I had witnessed a vision. I had seen the Heavenly Dimension. My souls energy had been risen so high that I was shown this sacred place, just like an Angel or spirit would do, only I am alive and here to tell you of this overwhelming experience! I wondered why there were no clouds in the sky there. Archangel Raphael then wrote, that there isn't any shadows or darkness in the Heavenly Dimension; everything is perfect, happy, positive, and most of all it is free of negativity! I hope I have satisfied your curiosity on what Angels actually do. Remember that Angels are all as one; they help guide our lives and help us in even the trivial little things, (such as getting your parking space remember). You might think that you don't need anyone to guide your life, as you may be independent and strong minded, but ask yourself, where do you get your courage and strength from? It isn't inherited. It isn't in your genes. It is your Guardian Angel and your other Angels, sending their miraculous golden rays from the Heavenly Dimension. They will guide you, and hold your hand down the correct pathway; in time of need your Angels will be there, even if you have committed a sin. Our Lord will not turn his back on you, he will simply send you an Angel to help heal your wounds, and heal the situation you find yourself in. So its not a question of what can Angels do? The question is what can Angels NOT DO!?

Chapter 14
Seeing Through The
Eyes Of An Angel

I am about to inform you with some miraculous news!! Us humans, no matter how Earth bound we may be, can see through the eyes of an Angel. As I have informed you all before, Angels can't see physically in our world. When the Angels told me of this experience on Earth when helping us out, I couldn't help but wonder what way they saw us, our trees and animals. Once again, all my Heavenly Angels heard my cry of never ending curiosity and they satisfied it right away!! (They are so patient, aren't they?) My family and I were all doing our every day things; my mother was sitting reading a book (she is a bookworm), my Earth Angel sister Olivia was grooming her wings, (I'm joking, she was making tea!) and I was talking a lot, as I normally do every day. It was just then when my mother just happened to glance up at the sky, and saw the sun an unusual white colour. She said that it actually looked more like the moon, and it seemed to be swirling round and round! She called us over to the window, and sure enough the sun was moving just like she said. It then seemed to get bigger, and change colour. It turned bright yellow, cerise pink, royal blue, a vivid green, then it went back to it's original white. The swirling movement was ongoing through this. It was so beautiful. What highlighted the whole experience, was the fact that we knew that we couldn't have normally looked at the sun directly, but here my family and I were, staring at it, without even the need of sun glasses!   (Remember though, this was a Heavenly gift for my family and I, and under no circumstances, should anyone look directly at the sun!.) Then I heard this soothing feminine voice in my mind. I knew instantly it was one of my Angels. she said "All of you, close your eyes". I told my mother and Olivia to do this and as we did, we could all see in our minds eye, the same vision!; there was the sun, bright orange, the sky was a cerise pink and the tree was outlined in black. Then the scene changed. It went blue, then green, the sky would change colour, the sun would change colour, it was the most beautiful thing we had ever witnessed. It was breathtaking!. Then everything became dark. We couldn't see the scene in our minds eye any longer. We wondered what it all meant. I then received an instant reply, and said "We were seeing through the eyes of an Angel". I didn't even know where I had gotten that information from. There I was in total amazement of what I was seeing, and I had an answer about it all without even having to think. Again I have to thank my Angels for their ongoing intelligence in sending such powerful information at such a fast pace!

As you may know, if you gaze at a candle flame for a period of time, then close your eyes, you will see colours. This was nothing like that. Everyone has experienced this to some degree, for example, with the bright flash of a camera etc, but this was overwhelming. Our Angels might not have the use of physical sight on our planet, but they can see everything clearly, just like us, only in the colours of the rainbow. The trees still move, the sun shines bright, the clouds still move along slowly, like a beautiful moving portrait! This is how our Guardian Angels see us here on planet Earth; my mother, Olivia and I appreciated that experience greatly, and have done every day since. Our Guardian Angels, see our souls in their unique way, moving along in our every day lives. After all what good would it be, having a Guardian Angel, if they couldn't see us, to save and guide us in whatever situation it may be. They see us perfectly, only in a much better light! Now your probably asking yourself "Can they see us at all times, even in the shower? Or even the bedroom?" Well aren't you all lucky to have such caring authors such as Olivia and I, to save your blushes! Our Angels cannot see our physical bodies, so if your taking a lovely bubble bath or a refreshing shower, do not fret! We are simply made up of colours in the eyes of Angels. We are like little floating blobs you'd see in a lava lamp! (Now you can relax, let your heart rate drop to normal again!) Our Guardian Angels need to be there, even when we're washing and grooming ourselves. After all, you never know what could happen. You could slip on a bar of soap in the shower, but (Hopefully not!) luckily, you have your Guardian Angel, to just simply slide that bar of soap out of your way to prevent an accident!

So our advice to you dear reader, is that if you want to see through the eyes of an Angel, look into the sky, and at the nature around you, and listen to your thoughts. The experience my family and I had was pretty unique. This incident was one of the reasons why the Angels guided us to write this book. The greatest pity for us though, is that everyone cannot have the same sight, at some point in their lives. However, God has provided us with the miracle of the natural world around us, to bring our minds to higher things. The detail, the organisation, and above all the colours, are truly amazing when you think about it. So the next time you look up into the sky and see a rainbow really look at it. Appreciate the beautiful colours within it, and try to realise, that God has provided this little piece of the Heavenly Realm to lift the heart, and fire the imagination. In a world where the media and society have our full attention firmly fixed on the material, our advice to you readers is this; take a few minutes to look out your window when you get up in the morning. The grass will be a healthy green, and the sky will always be blue. Look and listen to what is around you; a smile from someone you love, or the sound of your children's laughter. Appreciate these wonders because our world is a beautiful place, it is perfect. A focus on the material things will tend to make us forget that. Thank God for everything beautiful, that our world has to offer; Our Lords Angels do. Appreciate your colours, your life would be dull without them!

Chapter 15
If Only Time Didn't Exist

When was the last time you actually thought about time? Take a look at your family, and friends. Think back to happy memories you have of them, through your life. Seems like yesterday doesn't it? Our world revolves around time. There is always a certain time we have to be somewhere, we have a schedule to keep, planes to catch.....etc. Everything we do here on Earth, we put a time on it! The funny thing is, when it comes to the really important stuff, we think we have all the time in the world, for example, spending quality time with our family and friends, or developing our relationship with God. It would be good to refresh ourselves with the notion that we are just here on Earth for a little holiday, a vacation. Lets look at it this way. Olivia and I are only twenty two, and twenty years old respectively, but our connection with the Angelic Realm, has meant that we have a healthy appreciation of life. Now, a large part of this appreciation is, that we know we have a lot more to learn!. Maybe, though, if we didn't have a connection with the Heavenly Dimension, we would be like many other twenty-somethings, who think life is one big mess. We will admit sometimes, however, that we do think our lives are in a mess. Then we remember that there are other people out there in a much worse position than us, through illness, or some other circumstance. (Angelic Reasoning of course!) Our lives seem perfect compared to theirs, and truly they are. If the concept of time didn't exist in our world, I know it would be much easier on everyone; stressing about time, is the worlds favourite hobby. You might be thinking wait a minute, (Did you see what I did there!) I can't do that, I need to set my alarm clock in the morning to arrive at work on time!. Obviously, I don't expect you to put aside your career!. I would like you to think about a happy memory of a deceased loved one, that sits in the back of your mind. Something that makes you smile. You got one yet? Well hold that thought. Wouldn't it be glorious to re-live it? (Don't hesitate in doing so at this point) If you have thought of a wonderful memory you have shared with a deceased loved one, don't think that its wrong to do so. What is stopping you from taking this person to that certain place, at any time?. I agree, absolutely nothing! You can re-live that experience with your deceased loved one again and again, basically because they're watching over you, with care and guidance. To them, the concept of time that ruled them so much when alive, has simply vanished. They therefore, are able to be with you at *all* times. The chances are they are on your mind, because they wish to let you know that you can still enjoy their company. Keep them in your thoughts, and think of the time you shared together, re-live your memories with them. The Angels say that this is an example of how we humans can alter time itself in a way, as God gave each of us a mind that's capable of tapping in to past experience.

Another example which involves time, is if you haven't talked to an old friend in years. You miss them, but you're too busy to pick up the telephone and dial their number. What if something serious happened to this old friend of yours that you have been `meaning to call`? I am not going to create a feeling of guilt to sweep over your soul, but simply to awaken your senses. Could you handle the guilt associated with not making contact with your good friend, if they, for example, passed on? No you couldn't. I don't think anyone could. In reality, time gets too much attention here on Earth. A lot of us get so caught up on time, that we forget to live to our full potential. In the Heavenly Dimension, everyone has a different view. Time means nothing, simply because they have no day or night! They aren't rushing around trying to get things sorted, and getting all stressed. What are they doing? They are taking it easy. They are possibly doing what they didn't do here on Earth. Now, I know of many men and women that are dedicated to their work, but there is a limit! If you are Mr workaholic, that can't find enough hours in the day, or a Miss/Ms perfectionist, take a deep breath, and look at what your doing to yourselves! Sure, it is great that you have such dedication to your career, but what about your health? Are you getting enough sleep, nutrients, and most of all, care? The likelihood is that you are not, because you are causing so much stress on yourselves that, looking after yourself isn't on your 'to do' list. Most people in this sector of society (and there are hundreds of millions!) are going through life, forgetting how to live. The message from Heaven here is, don't push yourselves too far. Don't put a time on things. Sit back and relax. Work, yes, but try to enjoy it. Be grateful that you are able to do so; to clothe and feed yourself (and your family, depending upon your own circumstances of course!). The thing is, if you take a more relaxed view of the world, you will have plenty of time to fulfil your souls desires in this life; say all you need to, to your loved ones, see the world, or have fun with your kids as they grow up. Everyone is on their pathway in this life, but it can take a turn however, whether you want it to or not. Death seems so final here, to the vast majority of people in society, but it needn't be an issue to panic about. In reality, it is just a re-birth of your soul; it's a cleansing. My Angels have informed me of many unhappy souls who thought too much about time. They forgot what life really was about; they became ungrateful in many ways, as they didn't appreciate what God had given them to enjoy. In other words, they have died not saying and doing what they wanted to, because it wasn't the right TIME in their opinion. These kind of people can create problems for themselves, even when they pass over, like they did when they were alive. These souls are trapped between Earth and the Heavenly Dimension, because they have judged themselves when they died; they have thought that they were not worthy of entering the Heavenly Dimension, as their souls felt that they needed to do more when they were alive. This negativity is a blockage. Don't forget that your soul is made up of energy, so therefore it can be influenced in a positive or negative way, depending on how you feel when you pass over. The reason why I have written this chapter, is simply because the Angels have a wish to save a lot of you that have let time take over your lives. I am now going to ask you a question, and I want you to think about it. If you were to die right now, do you think you have lived your life for its highest good, and are worthy of entering the Heavenly Dimension? If your answer is no, well, I am grateful for your honesty. To those of you that said yes, two things come to mind. One, you may be one of those very rare people, who prays with complete thought for God, who does not judge or ridicule, and that loves completely, and with no thought of themselves. In this case, you are a credit to yourself, and to God. The second thought I have on this particular issue, is that your answer could be simply that your ego rules you, and that your opinion of yourself, could well be 'built on sand', so to speak. I am here to change your present outlook on the concept of death. Take your life at the moment. Is there anything you feel or have felt guilty about? There is? Well, get it off your mind. Get some help. Maybe you have hurt someone, talk to them, help them get over the pain you have caused. This might sound terrifying, but if you really think about it, wouldn't it be better not only for the person you have hurt, but most of all, yourself? Your conscience would be guilt free, therefore that potential negative blockage that could have held you back, has been transformed into a positive ray of golden light. This process is very important, and one which the Angels have told me to really talk about, as our misconceptions about time, as I have already said, mean that this sort of thing gets ignored. That is why I will go into this concept in a little more depth. I, personally, (Colleen) had a lot of people who hurt me in my past. I had carried grudges against these people for years, simply because I thought they had no right to make me feel worthless. If I was to re-live my child hood years in Primary and High School, I know now, that I would have tried to get to bottom of their reasoning. It has taken a long time (And the help of my Angels of course) to think the way I do, but I would try to help these people. I know what you may be thinking at this stage. How can someone, who was bullied by these people, really have made such a dramatic change in her outlook?. Well, its simple, because it wouldn't just be a case if me standing up for myself, but also offering to help the person who is truly in need, The Bully!. Therefore, the victim becomes the powerful strong defender ! Now, I am not directing you to cause conflict. I am advising a simple answer to a bullying problem; offering them help. If you are victim of bullies, I want you to stand up for yourself, and say what I would have said, because you do not want to carry the grudges that I did over the years, on certain people that hurt me. This is when my Angels came to the rescue. They told me to let go of the pain that people had caused in my life, send out a positive message to them, and most of all, forgive them. This is a difficult process, but it clears the negative blockages in your life and also helps and heals the person that you once hated. This could also save this person's possible guilt in later life, if they realise what they had done, as this could be a blockage of theirs. Proudly I can say, I have done so. My mind is at peace, and when I see any of the people that have hurt me, the old pain does not show. Believe it or not, I grew to like them, and in a way, to pity them, because the person who can hurt, is the person who is hurting the most. They cannot deal with their pain, so they pick on the happy pleasant people who they think deserve to suffer. So if you realise you may have been like that at any time, ask yourself Who is the one in need of help? I think you know the answer. I realise that this will take a lot of strength to do, but remember, your Angels are always with you. I ask for you to pray to Archangel Michael to cut away your negativity with his sword of Our Lord, and I also ask you to pray to Archangel Chamuel, to send you her powerful rays of strength and love. I used the example of my own experience with bullies, to demonstrate how, number one, you can help those who may have harmed you, by getting rid of negative thought patterns in both them, and yourself, and two, how the concept of time is only really relevant to the important things in life. The achievement of `Time Management` isn't as hard as you think. Just unwind a little, and take stock of your life. You will find that a pursuit of wealth, that is mercilessly tied to the clock, is not the way Heaven wants the World.

Life, in reality for each of us, will not last forever (On Earth anyway!). Do what you want with your life, appreciate your relatives and friends and even your enemies. When you come to that corner on your particular pathway, that takes you to the Heavenly Dimension, you do not want to be trapped between here and there. Forgive all who have hurt you, and send out love to all who have caused you pain. I promise you that Our lord will open his door. He will forgive everyone. Judging yourself is possible. I ask you not to do that, leave the judging up to Our lord. Set your alarm clock. Be on time, but most importantly, make time for your family and friends, and the building of your relationship with God, because our world hasn't got the advantage of having no day or night, like the Heavenly Dimension. Of course, I don't want you to forget that the concept of time exists. I want you to remember that there is still time to forgive and forget, and to direct your life to its highest good. Let golden light surround your lives and seep into your soul, because it will prove much more powerful than the black shadows that being caught up about time will produce. Let your hands of your clock tick normally, but be careful to *not let time tick away your life.*

Chapter 16
Is It Safe To Climb So High?

We all know how we feel about ourselves. If I was to ask you what your favourite part of your personality was, What would be your reply? Would you say "Well my personality's great, I'm a really good person, I help everyone, I never say a negative thing about anyone.." or, "I'm a good listener, I like helping people; sometimes I ridicule and judge people, but I regret it afterwards". Which reply is the correct one? Anyone who thinks that the first reply is correct, is a person with a high ego, who brags about their helping people; basically you are a glory hunter. If you are someone who agrees with the second reply, you are a person who likes to help if possible, and keep modest about it, therefore the second reply is correct. Take Jesus for example, He was the Son of God, He was sent down on Earth to help and heal us, He cured people with all sorts of illness; and even brought the dead back to life! He helped so many people, and changed so many lives, yet when He was crucified, He still took no credit for His actions. We all might think it is not easy to go by Our Lords way, but what exactly is so difficult about caring and loving people? Our Lord does not expect us to try and live up to the standards He had, when He was here on Earth. That is impossible. He was and is God. It isn't such a hard task though, when you think about it. The vast majority of people here on Earth however, follow a different pattern of action; the abuse of Alcohol, Sexual misconduct, Mental and Physical abuse of the weak, and the Ridicule of our neighbour. This is not Our Lords way, it is Lucifer's. So many of us here on Earth, seem to be able to carry out the negative more easily, than the positive. What a lot of you don't see, is that Lucifer's way may be 'cool', and make you feel good at the time, but truthfully, you are obeying his advice and ruining yourself. The following of this way of life can be viewed as egotistical in the extreme. A lifestyle that punishes your body, and in turn makes life difficult for those around you, or that love you, is very selfish. Now, you could argue that you have Free Will, and that your lifestyle is in your control. That is indeed true; God gave all of us Free Will to do the right thing. He didn't, however mean that everyone could poison their bodies and minds in a selfish way, that brings heartache and strife for all concerned. God wants you to have everything possible (within reason!) The trick is to have a balance that will keep your ego in check. Olivia and I drink alcohol. (Yes that's correct, the Earth Angel drinks!). We are all human after all. We can have a few drinks, no problem, but we are mindful that we cannot take advantage of alcohol. Having a drink is our vice, if you like. We have however, exceeded the safe amount on a few occasions, and paid the price! However, if we were to do this all the time at the expense of family, and work commitments, we would be at the mercy of a high ego. Its great for all of us to have confidence and love ourselves, but to 'Be in love ' with yourself is vanity, and that's a sin. Now, I'm not only getting at us women, I'm also referring to all you men out there. I don't expect all the women reading this book to stop buying cosmetics, (believe me I couldn't separate with that side of vanity either) and as for you men, I don't expect you to stop buying your hair gel or favourite after shave. The Angels ask for us to be at peace with ourselves. Have confidence, but don't take advantage of the fact you may look good, and that people admire you. Letting it all go to your head, will only raise you up the 'Ego-ladder' the Angels told us about. Well let me explain. Archangel Raphael delivered a message about the ego. He sketched (Through me of course!), a ladder with twenty steps. The safe point in the ladder is step number thirteen. When I say "safe", I mean that this is the point where you are at peace with yourself and love yourself but not getting obsessed about how you look and making others feel bad as a result. Archangel Raphael's opinion is that everyone is beautiful on Earth; he said that we all have a beauty about us, whether its our smile or our laughter. We all must have confidence to get through life, because if we didn't, we would be really unhappy! So don't think Our Lord wants us to walk around saying "Oh I don't love myself, I hate everything about me" he wants us to walk proud, be confident, but not to intimidate others while doing so. Are you safer at the top of a ladder, way up high, looking down on people, or are you safe in the middle, not to high and not to low? You certainly are not safe at the bottom of the ladder either, because basically your looking up at everyone. No one is going to notice the person standing last in line. If your stuck at the bottom of the ladder, you've nowhere to go. So stay in the middle of the ladder. For those of you who are confident, I am pleased that you are happy with your body, your life and your personality. For those of you who have so much confidence you store it in little bottles in your bedroom, I want you to sit back and look at your self. Imagine someone acting out an attitude similar to your own. Could you handle having a conversation with someone like that? You may find that there will be things you won't like about this person; overconfidence can be very `in-your-face` for most people. If you (or someone who has read this) conclude(s) that you are in this category, I ask you to ask for Archangel Uriel's help. He will calm you, and help this attitude. He will also help you to express yourself in other ways, and not just focus upon the cosmetic. For those who have very low self esteem, try this out. I want you to make a list of good and bad points about yourself. Then, get a close friend to do the same about you as a person. You'll find that your friend will have many more positive points on

their list about you, than you may have on your own. Pray to Archangel Raphael to heal your emotional wounds; he waits upon everyone with his healing heart, ready to help as soon as he is asked. The Heavenly Golden Ladder is a great test of ones ego. It tells no lies, it speaks only of the truth. Some of us say to have perfect confidence is to be perfect. This is not true. Total perfection is not reality. We are on planet Earth, no one here is perfect. We have both negative and positive energies in our bodies, it is up to us within ourselves which energy is higher. Stay optimistic and positive, and your life will shine bright. Think of the humble dog; its life is ordinary just like any other animal, but it is up to the dog whether or not he chooses to wag his tail. Do you prefer a happy dog or a fierce one? Everyone wants to be the happy dog of course. Since we are human, we have no tail to wag to express our happiness and optimism, but we do have our smiles, so keep on step thirteen of the golden ladder, do not go no higher or lower and you will remain one happy go lucky puppy!

Chapter 17
The Angels Use of Colour
Within Our chakras

Do you know what your chakra points are? You Don't? Well, never fear, this chapter will enlighten you about the whole issue of these energy points, and of how the Angels work through them. Olivia and I were pretty uninformed about the placement, and purpose of chakras, but our Heavenly friends have given us a very comprehensive knowledge. So, what we will deliver in this chapter, is a run-down of the chakra points, their use to our physical and emotional well-being, and the colours the Angels use in each. The Archangels take charge of this issue, and each rules their own chakra point. There are seven main chakras throughout the body. They have a shape not unlike a lotus flower, with all the many petals made up of the same energy, and rotate like a fan at all times. When these energy points are blocked or unbalanced, this means that they are rotating in an anti-clockwise direction. Depending upon the person, the speed of this rotation varies. If you are a spiritual, open minded person, they probably spin at a fast pace, if you are a person who is ignorant to spiritual experiences then your chakras are likely to be spinning much more slowly. These chakras are placed throughout our bodies, in a straight line from the top of the head, to the base of the body. They are as follows:

The crown chakra:

The crown chakra is placed on the very top of the head. The purpose of having a chakra point here, is so we can connect spiritually to the Heavenly Dimension and Spirit World. This is where our energies connect to the highest of Archangels and Angels; in other words, the crown chakra is our key to open the door to other dimensions. The colour of this chakra is violet, has a connection to Archangel Zadkiel. This Archangel will help you to see the divine light in all areas of your life. He uses a violet ray of energy, just like our crown chakra, to do his work. If you are a person in a relationship, or business partnership that you are very unhappy and confused in, pray to Archangel Zadkiel. He will release your stress and balance your crown chakra with his powerful violet energy, and dispose of all negativity in the head area. So, if your suffering from stress, ask of his help and you will receive a glorious violet cleansing.

The third eye chakra:

Moving down the body, the next chakra is our third eye, (Also known as the minds eye) The third eyes purpose is to enable us to form a connection to those parts of Our Lords creation which are invisible in our world, such as fairies and Angels. Your third eye chakra is an indigo colour, and is placed in the middle of the forehead between your eyes. When your third eye chakra is unbalanced, you tend to suffer from headaches, mental anxiety, sinus problems etc. This is where Archangel Jophiel can help. His indigo coloured energy will help alleviate problems in this area, and open your mind to wisdom and ongoing knowledge. His assistance is always available to you, and he will send his divine indigo light throughout your third eye chakra, for your little flower to spin in the correct direction. (but don't throw away your painkillers).

The throat chakra:

This chakra is placed in the throat area. A lot of us have emotional issues hidden within this chakra, as we can tend to not speak up about things that annoy us. This will automatically leave the chakra unbalanced, leading to a sore throat in many cases. The colour of our throat chakra is blue. Archangel Michael who works with the blue ray, can cut away any negativity from this chakra, (and no his sword won't cut your vocal cords, so keep calm!) He will give you strength and help you deal with any problems we are dealing with. He will surround you with a light of courage, to speak of your true feelings, and your throat chakra will be cleared and spinning as normal. So don't hold things back. Tell people what you are truly feeling. Even if your friend buys something `beautiful`, which is actually hideous, be honest and speak the truth. Honesty is a great quality, and you will find, it also is a great cure for a sore throat!

The heart chakra:

This chakra dwells within the heart area. This is where we keep our expressions of love, and where we get our inspiration from. For example, Olivia plays her music from her heart; her talent is highlighted, as she puts thoughts and feelings into it. The heart chakra can also have negative areas, which we keep hidden; for example, if you find it difficult to express love to loved ones or partners. It has a green coloured energy associated with it, which Archangel Raphael is connected to very strongly. Ask for his help, and he will heal any blockage to expressing your feelings towards others. Archangel Raphael works with a green glorious healing ray, which he introduces into the chakra, to clear our negativity. He can even heal a broken heart! We all know how bad that can be, don't we?

The solar plexus:

This chakra dwells in the stomach area. This is placed in the centre of our bodies above our navel (belly button). The importance of keeping this chakra balanced, is that all our abdominal organs are controlled by it. This can also be where some of us keep aggression. For example, if someone ever caused you to feel really angry and stressed, or if you were very stressed in your life generally, would you ever feel nausea or a burning sensation in that area? Well, this circumstance, for instance, can lead your solar plexus chakra to become unbalanced. This is a most important chakra to keep balanced, as our body organs' normal functions are vital to health. Archangel Gabriel rules this chakra. He works on a gold/white ray (Which is the same colour as the chakra itself) He will release all of your pain and negativity from the abdominal area, and his light energy will lift your physical energy also, giving you a spring in your step!

The Sacral chakra:

This chakra is placed in our lower abdomen. It is an orange/pink colour, and is ruled by Archangel Chamuel. This chakra is connected to our sexual energies. A blockage can occur here, if you don't keep the correct balance within your sexual activities. Too much, or indeed, too little, can upset the chakra's fine balance, and physical ailments, such as kidney infection, bladder trouble, or maybe a complete stop in the function of your reproductive organs may occur. I advise you to ask Archangel Chamuel for assistance, if you find yourself with problems in this area. She is connected to the emotional lower abdomen, and works with a powerful pink/orange ray, which will clear all the blockages causing your physical symptoms. If you are sexually detached, and feel anxiety about it, she will release your blockages and soothe any frustrations you may have. This however, happens purely on a spiritual level. Archangel Chamuel will help you in this whole area, but the partner you may require, you will have to find yourself!

The base chakra:

This is known as the root chakra. This is placed in the genital area of our bodies. Strangely enough, the purpose of this chakra is not involved with our sexuality, rather, it hinges upon us having a balanced personality, and deals with our ambition. This chakra's colour is red. When our root chakra is blocked, a fear of letting our true personality shine out, can occur. A lot of people have this problem, which can last their whole lives, as so many people have to feel comfortable with someone, before they let them know what they are truly like. If you have found that you are always having difficulty in dealing with people, or that you have confidence problems within your personality, I ask you to seek assistance from Archangel Uriel. He works with ruby ray which also contains gold. He will free you from your fear of others, and their reactions towards your true identity as a person. Ask for him to surround you with a glorious ruby red light, to help shine out the wonderful personality that God gave each one of us.

I hope you can now understand why we relate our chakras with our Archangels because there are seven chakras, correct? And there are also seven Archangels. They all use rays of light which are coloured to suit the chakra which they are strongly connected to. We need our chakras to be in balance, for our spiritual and physical well-being. So, if you find you have an emotional, physical, or indeed, spiritual blockage within you, ask the Archangels to help, heal, and guide you, to help soothe your problems. So when you see a rainbow, the colours within it are a reflection and reminder, that the Archangels, with their rays of light, are always there above you, ready to help; all you have to do is ask.

Chapter 18
Co-operative Spirits

When here on Earth, we are surrounded by Spirits, Angels, and Archangels. Most of us are ignorant to the existence of the scope of the Heavenly Dimension, yet do you know that as you read this book, you are probably sitting along side one of your deceased relatives and loved ones. (Don't throw our book down!) Relax , they probably know you; they are your relatives and friends, people who you once laughed and maybe even cried with! Spirits can appear displaying a range of emotions; patient, anxious, negative, positive, angry , happy, humorous and even aggressive. I have had experience with only with a few of the above. Fortunately, a lot of the spirits that contact me are positive and very happy. You may be thinking "Then why do they contact you?" Well, when your loved ones pass over to the Heavenly Dimension, they still watch over your lives, almost like they are sitting behind a one-way mirror, looking in on you. We are visible to them and we are at the other end, looking at what we think is a normal every day mirror, but really we are looking into a face of a deceased loved one!!! My main reason on writing this chapter, is basically that a lot of you out there don't quite have enough knowledge about spirits. They are not all evil. That's how the media portray them. They are not in your homes because you need to pray more. People always jump to that conclusion, and think "Oh my, maybe we aren't praying enough" Well sorry to tell you, but you are wrong!! Its almost the same as your relatives that are physically here, coming in for a cup of tea and a chat! That's pretty normal isn't it? Well spirits are the same, only you don't have to boil the kettle and worry about not having anything nice in your larder!!! Relief I'd say?? ☺

So what is it about Spirits that terrifies all of us here? Is it the fact that we have buried them, said our goodbyes and thought that they were gone for good?(In a hole in the ground, or cremated and sitting in an Urn on your mantle piece?) Death is so final to us all, but you should know it's a rebirth! Our world is an illusion to the Heavenly Dimension. I'm sure you have heard that spirits can walk through walls? Well this is why. They walk through walls, our doors, chairs, our furniture and material goods…etc. These are all an illusion to spirits. Its like us breezing through a door made of tissue paper. You could do it easily!. I have had many visits from spirits, mainly with messages to pass on to my relatives, or close friends, as being a music teacher, I knew that if I had made it public, it would have damaged my career. After all, who wants to send their child to a spiritual worker that communicates with the deceased? (Although I do think that people might notice now. Do you think anyone will notice? Hope not!) Anyway back to the deceased! As I was saying, I have had many experiences with all sorts of spirits; some that are trapped between the Heavenly Dimension and here, some that are happy and want to tell their families they watch over them, and then of course there are the negative souls, that just don't want to leave! I asked my mother one day to inform her friend to look out for some classical music pieces, as she regularly attended car boot sales. I had some luck. My mothers friend found some great pieces from the German composer Handel! The pieces were inside this little old brown suitcase, old and stained yellow with age. I played some of the pieces, finding them quite easy, after having some fourteen years experience playing some highly challenging classical pieces, my aunt Lily had introduced me to. There was so much more behind each piece I played though. It was almost like someone was standing beside me, listening. A few days later, I looked at the little suitcase and I saw a woman, with her hair up in a bun ,wearing a long purple skirt, maroon cardigan and cream blouse underneath. She wasn't looking directly at me though. It was almost like she was talking to someone behind me. I then seen Archangel Raphael all in my minds eye, putting his hand out towards her, to take her to the light. Apparently she was trapped, and was going about her own business, like she did when she was physically here on Earth! When I had opened the little case first, I got a strong smell of a musky perfume. Now, I can open that little brown case without the smelling the scent, as she is no longer attached to it. She had left it behind, and moved on to the Heavenly Dimension, where she should have arrived many years ago! This is what I would call a negative spirit. The reason I say this is basically, because she was unhappy. She was walking around in her own time, and couldn't find any of her loved ones. You may question the whereabouts of the Angels in this case. Well, the Angels can only help those who want to be helped. I have asked Archangel Raphael why there are many here that have suffered great pain emotionally and physically, help seemed to be absent from their Guardian Angel. Archangel Raphael stated that those who do not want help and have no faith, block their Guardian Angels out with their negativity. They let the darkness in and block the light. This does not mean that this person is bad. These people I sympathize with, for they didn't place any faith in religion or their Angels; they basically need our prayer, so when you pray at night, squeeze in a little prayer for those in need.

If you have seen, or even dreamt of a deceased loved one, this is their way of saying hello. It may even be their scent that is familiar to you. Again this is a way of letting you know that they are there, and not six feet under or on your mantle piece! A visit from a spirit even if not a relative is glorious; there are co-operative spirits, they do exist. Not all are standing behind you, ready to write boo on your steamed bathroom mirror. I know of every kind of spirit you could possibly think of, and even the evil ones aren't as terrifying as they sound! They are just angry and confused that they are lost, so they take it out on the living. Put yourself in their shoes. It would be irritating wouldn't it? If decent people exist why shouldn't decent spirits? As my father would say, it isn't the dead you have to worry about, it's the living! My advice to you readers with this chapter is, basically change your outlook on what you call the deceased. They have names, they can see every day what goes past in our lives, and not all are evil. Try not to picture your deceased loved ones as a walking corpse, any time you may get a reading done with a psychic, try and see them as they were here on Earth, because that is truly what they are like in the Heavenly Dimension, only much more fulfilled! Look at what they have left behind, and imagine them in a wonderful green open garden, with all the fruit they can eat, full of love and a sparkle in their eye which has gotten brighter! Spirits are people. Respect the deceased like you would the living. We are only here on a holiday don't forget. Every good thought which is sent out, has a golden reward for you in the Heavenly Dimension! It isn't the question of "Do spirits exist", it's the question "Did your loved ones exist?". Your answer is yes to both of those questions! Why would something that Our lord created, die forever when it can relive like the seeds of any flower can bloom every year, even though you have only planted them once!

Chapter 19
From Non Believers To Beyond Believers

I have had many experiences with many of my clients. Some have been overwhelming , exciting, and intriguing; others have been so negative that I've just wanted to get up from my seat, and run out of the room. These people were sending out such an over powering negative energy, they blocked me from helping them deliver their Angels guidance, and their deceased relatives kind words of comfort. This often occurs when the person is a "non believer". I can and must accept people with this attitude and outlook about the after life, past lives etc, as they are the people that I need to reach out to and touch. They are the people that Our Lord wants us to save! They are ignorant to such glorious experiences, ongoing help and guidance, and the contentment they can feel from their Guardian Angels and deceased loved ones. If they were to only open their hearts, they would never feel alone, but most importantly, much happier within themselves; because your heart feels, your heart is where you feel these emotions physically. Many people cannot feel such emotion, because their hearts are blocked to love, consideration and even hurt. This causes difficulty giving and receiving love; some people don't want to get hurt. Its not that anyone wants to experience emotional pain, but personally, I think you need to experience hurt, in order to appreciate love and positivity on an emotional level. You will often find as you get on in life, you will begin to show gratitude for the good people you meet; so many you will meet will prove to be unkind, and not appreciative of you as a person. This, unfortunately, can also be applied to the relationship I have with some of my clients. I meet some people who lock the doorway to their hearts; they bolt it up, add chains, and maybe even hammer a few six inch nails in for good measure. They do this in case this crazy person before them with sixth sense`, may actually *see* something about them that they want to keep personal. (Even though they secretly wish that they get given a large amount of information) They sit there, petrified, thinking, "I'll hammer a few extra nails here around my heart, to set an even bigger challenge, see if she can read me now, ha !"

Yes, indeed this is the attitude many of my clients have had. Can you even begin to imagine, how difficult it would be to help and read, with that attitude? Those who want to be read, I can manage blind folded, with my hands tied behind my back (not that I want to be tested with such a challenge!). These people are my favourite. Pleasant and co-operative. I've often thought though, that these people aren't the clients that really need my message, these are the people who listen with me and not to me. These people are already blessed with a faith in the Heavenly Dimension; they accept it with no misconceptions, or questions about proof. They just believe that it is there, just as they believe in God. I needed to change the people who suffered from the highly contagious disease, called scepticism! Everyone loves a challenge. Well, I as a fire sign, love challenges, (Typical Arian! Don't you agree Olivia!)

I have been challenged by many clients, wondering Where, Why, Who and What? I am now going to tell you of an experience I had with one client, that suffered greatly from scepticism, but thankfully she was cured by the golden touch!

One evening I got a phone call from a neighbour of mine, who asked if I could take one of her good friends for a reading. She seemed quite intrigued by me, and of what I seemed capable of. I agreed to take her as a client. When that evening finally came, my client sat before me. She seemed to be on edge, but I could sense she had mixed feelings about what was to happen; almost like she planned to dismiss what I had to say before I had said it! I asked her what guidance she would like from her Angels. She said she had a few questions; she asked them, but not directly. The way she questioned, left me puzzled. She was testing me, I had no doubt of it. She had asked me about an experience she had a few years back, for her Angels to tell her what it was, even though she had full knowledge of it already. When I read the answer that the Angels had given me, her eyes widened. She almost glared at me. I asked if she was ok. She accused me of doing research on her, to be able to give her such detail. I sat there thinking "Oh no, not another one". When it came to her card reading, I found her quite difficult to read. She blocked me with each piece of information I gave her. She fired back with, "How do you know that?", or "Who told you that?". Her negative energy blocked the flow of information I was receiving. So I closed my deck of cards, took my pencil in my hand again, to lean on the Angels. I wanted to let her know that I was genuine, to leave her calm, and help her with her problems. She tested me once again, but I was unaware this time, as she had asked the Angels for an affirmation for her friend, to help her with a problem she was having. Of course the Angels gave her good friend the guidance she needed, and when the reading was finished she got up, and I shook her hand and thanked her for coming. I noticed she stared at me strangely then; as I watched her leave my home that evening, I knew I would hear from her again. (Firstly she was shocked, and secondly, she suffered from chronic scepticism). Those who don't believe and are complete sceptics, when `converted`, don't seem to fully grasp it to begin with, but after a day or two when they finally give in, a new pathway they begin to walk, will always bring them back for more.

My thinking was right. She contacted me again within the next few days, full of apology, saying that she couldn't believe her thought pattern the night we spoke, and the way she had doubted me in my work. I asked her, what changed her views? She then told me that the affirmation that the Angels had given her good friend, really related to her life, and that the whole experience sent shivers up her spine. It took that client of mine to ask for help for another and not herself, to truly accept what she was seeing, and hearing. She was a challenge no doubt, but one that I succeeded in, one that I *needed* to succeed in, and with the help of Our Lords creation the Angels, I had done so.

Proudly I have to say I have `converted` all of those who were so inclined, that came to me for readings, into believers. In fact, I made such a good job in converting them, that they even began to think beyond believing. It's not always what you see physically that matters, it's what you feel, and what you allow your temple to experience. You are the holder of the key to all your door ways; you choose which door to open, and which to lock. I ask you to be brave. Unlock some doors, and let that part of your soul experience freedom. The whole sphere of the Heavenly Dimension, and the influence it all has on us, is beyond belief. Olivia, my family and I, have seen and heard things that many people would find very hard to believe. This book has been written to tell the world of our experience, and provide evidence to sceptics, that the Angels want to help and guide us, that the deceased want to connect with us, and that God loves us at all times.

Chapter 20
Lets Put Out That
Miraculous Light

Your probably wondering, Why would anyone want to put out a miraculous light? I myself have asked the same question. I'm not talking about lights in the cities, vehicles, homes or Christmas tree lights, I'm talking about the light that shines within us all as people, the light of God, the light of Life, the light in you! When I refer to each of us having a light within us, please do not imagine a light bulb or a candle flame, as this light uses no electricity. The light within us, comes from our pure side, from giving love, and listening to those who need a shoulder to lean on, or exchanging presents on special occasions. This is where the light within us all shines brighter than at any other time, as we are all doing something positive for those around us. Even being supportive to a friend in an argument; (not that we should get a kick out of conflict), but just knowing you've helped that person, will make you feel good within yourself. Therefore, your light will shine brighter in these special moments. Some of us have helped so many people in the world, and put so much time into healing their lost souls. Don't you hate it though, when they become healed, but come back with this "I don't need you" attitude?. Then you start doubting yourself as a person, and think you have done something wrong? STOP THAT RIGHT NOW! The only people in the wrong here are the people that you helped heal, the people that took advantage of your kind nature, and then when they were finished draining every ounce of goodness you have they throw you into the trash can! Sounds harsh I know, but very true. Throughout these past few years since I've came to terms with my gift, I noticed that people I had known for years, started opening up to me about their very personal and most private lives. At first, I'll admit, I thought it was great. The advice I had given always had a great outcome, which was strange, for the lack of experience I had had in my life, with relationships and travel etc. Of course, I was just a very normal young girl, that was being given information by my Angels and Spirit Guides. In the beginning, I didn't mind comforting those with my words that came to me for guidance, as I hate to see unhappiness in anyone, but I noticed, the more time I spent with these people that I knew so well, the more effort I put in, began to change them. They grew stronger in mind, yes, which I thought was great, but after a while, they didn't speak to me like they used to. They tried to undermine me, as now they felt so much better, they're previous 'weakness' (In their opinion), made them angry, as they felt they shouldn't have needed to be counselled by someone so young. This is where the people I thought had faith in me as a person, became my enemies, as they had chose to do so, without knowing that Lucifer had given them front row tickets to see his play, on how he would kill off ones self esteem. This past year, I have helped a lot of people with their lives; from broken homes to suicides, and everything in-between. This news, which my family and I think is wonderful, had gotten around by word of mouth throughout the locality. People began to talk, but the conversations these people were having weren't very pleasant. In fact, the people in my area who were practically strangers to me, had much nicer words to speak of me than my own blood. This is when doubt began to seep into my mind. My self esteem crept so low that I thought to myself "I don't want to do this anymore". These gossiping idiots were killing off my confidence within myself not only about my gift with my Angels, but the confidence within myself as a person. My positive personality vanished. The miraculous light, that had been given to me by Heaven, was on its way out. My optimism had vanished, until the fifth day within the week this all happened, I craved for my paper and pencil, and I knew I had to satisfy it. Once I had done so, the message stated " *You must stand with your feet firmly on the ground, you are blessed with a true gift that some are blind to seeing, as Lucifer has attacked many humans that surround you which you have once healed, because you had made them strong. So strong, they could then make their own decisions which just happened to be the wrong one. When you are to confront these people, do not look at them with disappointment but with strength, stability and with a win win attitude, FORGIVE THEM because they do not know of what they are doing"*

When I read this message at the time, I knew instantly, that my Angels were warning me that I was being attacked by Lucifer, as I was comforting so many people, sharing the light within me, and helping them re-light theirs. That infuriated him. All his hard work failed; the depression, the anxiety that these people had once suffered vanished as I helped them, they began to grow passionate about their work, and strong within themselves as people. His plan then, was to send out negativity to attack me mentally, which he succeeded in temporarily, as I doubted my gift. Lucifer wanted me to stop carrying out my good deeds for those whom I cared for, and wanted to save, which meant that if the public doubted me, then my self esteem would have went downhill, and I wouldn't have wanted to practice anymore. Thankfully my Angels saved me with that message! I stood firmly on my own two feet and made a promise to myself that I would never let others negativity seep into my soul again. I have kept that promise and always will. Our world needs more people with a giving attitude. I'm not talking materially. I'm talking about people with considerate hearts, to help others in need; to help someone cross the road, stop judging, put a stop to ridicule, giving someone a compliment about themselves as a person, telling them their qualities etc. This is where you then shine your light upon others, then their light within shines brighter like a calm candle flame. I ask of you to always keep your light within on, never switch it off, as it isn't going to put your electric bill sky high, set your house on fire, or give you heartburn. You will only experience warmth and contentment when you send out that light. You will receive the biggest beam of light you can imagine reflecting back at you from the Heavenly Dimension for carrying out a glorious deed, so I say SWITCH IT ON!

Hello readers!

Your Probably thinking this is quite peculiar, with the authors interrupting your quiet reading time! We offer you, dear readers, our greatest apologies, but we thought we would warn you in advance, that this book is now coming to an end. What better way could we complete this book other than ending it with a fairy tale! We are now going to tell you a true tale of love, as pure and ongoing as a waterfall, and to open the hearts of our readers that have let the magic of love and fairy tales fade in their lives.

Live life with a dream like attitude, let fairies and Angels dance at your bedside,

110

let the leprechauns grant your three wishes, bring your relationship with God to new Heights, whatever you believe Him to be, and widen not only your children's outlook on magical happenings, but your oldest and dearest friends!

We hope you have enjoyed our book. Thank-you for buying it. If you found this an exciting read; don't worry, the next one's almost done!

Yours sincerely

Colleen & Olivia xoxo

♥

Chapter 21
Why Love is One Big
Jigsaw Puzzle!

Almost every human being on this planet has asked themselves "Does true love exist?". I bet 50% of our readers have sighed and said "yes" and the other 50% have moaned and said "Oh come on, no way!" Well I am here today, to introduce two people that are so in love they actually have to pinch themselves, to see if they are living in the real world, because it all seems too good to be true. So good in fact, that they both contact each other at nearly every hour of the day, to make sure they both feel exactly the same way from the last time they spoke! I am now going to tell you a true fairy-tale, about two wonderful people who have experienced love at first sight!

Once upon a time, a fair haired Earth Angel was scheduled to carry out a healing on a tall, dark, handsome male whom she was introduced to, by her cousin. She was asked if she could take him as a first time client; they knew absolutely nothing about each other except, that he was to relax, and she was to heal his mind and body. Before the dark client arrived at the Earth Angels home that day, she waited with great patience as she had done so many times before with other clients, and prayed that it would all go well. Little did she know, that   when that client walked through the door, she would simply crumble like a chocolate chip cookie!. As he entered the room, he was gazing down towards his feet. He then ran his fingers over his chin, and glanced up at her to make eye contact. The dark client looked at this woman in awe; his heart grew almost twice its size, but yet he remained coy, and tried to control his breathing. The Earth Angels dark client, had no idea that the feeling was very mutual!

The Earth Angel gazed upon her client in her healing room as she was carrying out her duty as an Integrated Energy Therapist. As she brushed his arms, she felt every hair on her arms and neck stand straight up; this was a feeling of excitement and rushed emotion all at once, she couldn't quite put her finger on it. She certainly couldn't kiss her client to find out why she was feeling this as it would be inappropriate doing such a thing in her profession!(But she really felt the need!)

When his IET treatment had came to an end, he thanked her and left, both smiling at each other, yet trying their hardest to remain calm physically, even though mentally they were both thinking such bizarre thoughts of each other. An hour after her dark client left that day, she thought she would phone her cousin just to make sure he was satisfied with his treatment, and with this Earth Angel being so dedicated to her work, she thought she must always make sure her client was content, (In other words, she was checking up on her dark client to see if he had mentioned anything about her personally, and not professionally). The Earth Angels cousin, told her how his good friend had felt, and decided to match them up on a date, especially when he found out that she was feeling exactly the same. The Earth Angel jumped with excitement! She met her dark client once again, only this time he wasn't her client, and she certainly wasn't in professional mode. She was being highly flirtatious; her dark client doing exactly the same. They both laughed, exchanged shy smiles, and phone numbers by the end of the night. They had arranged to meet up the next day, as they were both experiencing feelings that were such a shock to their systems. They couldn't sleep, eat, or even speak when they were separated, and yet they had just met? Can you even begin to imagine the torture they both felt?. This confusing energy that was created between them both, and yet it was so addictive they couldn't part with it!

But sadly they had to part. They only had those two dates. The Earth Angel had received a message, that it wasn't the correct timing in her life to settle into a relationship so soon after just separating from another. She had to know deep inside that it was love she was feeling, and not a feeling of fear from being alone and on the rebound. She informed her dark client that she could not see him any longer. He was devastated. Being the wonderful person he is, he said he understood and that he wished her the very best for the future, and in her career. He even wished her the best in her love life, and yet he thought he would never be a part of it. His heart mourned and so did hers but it wasn't to be. It wasn't the pathway they were to take; they had to go their separate ways, it saddened them both deeply, even though it only lasted forty eight hours. They thought of each other every day after that for 360 days, until they were to be re-united by the Angels again exactly one year later, but only this time for eternity! The Earth Angel told him the great news that she received from her Guardian Angel, and they met up that evening for a few drinks to celebrate. Even though there was alcohol present, they were both intoxicated with love for each other. That long year apart had came to an end. They were to be together now only, because it was all to do with "divine timing". The first time round, was not the right time for them to be together as an item, as they had both so much to do in that year, (so many problems to sort out, negativity to clear, and clutter in their lives before joining as one). When they had done so, they were re-united with each other once again in harmony. In that year they both felt torn from each other, as if a piece of them was missing. The Angels informed me that soul mates do exist, and once they have met, they experience the most overwhelming feeling. Their minds go blank. They think nothing but of each other, and then when they are apart, they feel almost physically sick! As we all know when building a jigsaw puzzle, the picture is never going to be complete without the last piece, to add the finishing touch. This works exactly the same with us. Our souls are like jigsaw puzzles and when we meet our partner that we are to spend eternity with, we fit together like one jigsaw piece fits into another, and we feel complete. We can then begin to build another jigsaw puzzle, about our new life that we are to build as one. We fit the pieces together. It is our duty to find any lost or broken pieces, and put them back together. I hope you have enjoyed reading this true tale and yes the Earth Angel is Olivia!

I ask of you to pray to Archangel Chamuel, if you are a person who is longing to meet their soul mate. She will guide you to him/her, and when you finally meet, you will know instantly that they are for you. Not just for a fling, but for a life long swing; the rope will never rot, and neither will your wooden seat, you shall sit on your seat, and your partner shall push you high and catch you if you fall, and with one kiss, make the whole world seem a brighter place. When one is to be in love it's terrific, for ones love to last forever, is miraculous. Open your arms and you shall receive love, because everyone truly deserves a loving companion on Earth. Our Lord wants each and every one of us to discover our soul mate. He has planned for you both to meet, but only He has put in a few boobie traps along the way, for your own good. Those few mistakes that you will have to make, will make you the person you are today. Never regret that you have been with any ex partners, because without the experience with them as people, you wouldn't appreciate the true love that you meet. It is only then you discover that love conquers all, and we all live happily ever after!

~

In Loving Memory Of Our Grandfather
Peter Coney, May He Rest In Peace.

~

The History Of The Child Of Prague

The devotion of the Holy Child Jesus has been a tradition of the Catholic Church since the middle ages. The city of Prague, in what is now modern Czechoslovakia has had a very chequered history. The origin of this particular image of the Infant Jesus, came from a vision a monk received depicting the Nativity. His influence brought about the making of a wax statue, that was dressed in real robes. Devotion to the statue became widespread, and the city enjoyed prosperity and safety. However, after a period of time, people began to move away from veneration of the little icon, and war broke out. The city was taken by an army that desecrated all the Churches. Amazingly, though damaged, the statue was found in the ruins of the Church it had been on display. A return to the adoration of the Blessed Infant, brought the city back to life after further war, but throughout history, the fortunes of the city and its inhabitants has been closely linked. Devotion to the Blessed Infant of Prague has become widespread all over the world. This devotion is a veneration of our Lord's sacred Infancy. Many Saints had been strongly dedicated to the Divine Child such as, St Anthony of Padua, St. Francis of Assisi and St. Teresa of Avila. The statue of the most Holy child wears a white under shirt, over it a white rocheta, then a silk top with frills around the neck and hands. Finishing with the last garment is a red gown which is like the priest's pluvial. On his head is placed a crown, in his left hand he holds a globe of the world and in his right giving the sign of peace, stating peace on Earth. Many of those that has worshipped the statue of the most Holy Child have received many healings, graces, blessings and favours. As the Holy Child once stated, "Have pity on Me and I will have pity on you, the more you honour Me , the more I will bless you".

It is a known Irish tradition for those who pray to the Child of Prague to set the statue outside their home the night before their wedding in hope for good weather on their joyful day.

Printed in the United States
47049LVS00001B/16-204